Roadside Wildflowers

of the Southern Great Plains

Roadside

University Press of Kansas

Wildflowers

of the Southern Great Plains

Craig C. Freeman & Eileen K. Schofield

Published by the University Press of Kansas
(Lawrence, Kansas 66045), which was
organized by the Kansas Board of Regents and
is operated and funded by Emporia State
University, Fort Hays State University, Kansas
State University, Pittsburg State University, the
University of Kansas, and Wichita State
University

Printed in Hong Kong

10 9 8 7 6 5 4 3 2 1

The paper used in this publication meets the
minimum requirements of the American
National Standard for Permanence of Paper for
Printed Library Materials Z39.48-1984.

Illustrations

All drawings of plants were done by Eileen K.
Schofield. Maps were prepared by Vera Sehon,
Graphic Arts Service, Center for Research,
Inc., University of Kansas.

Photographs

Page numbers on which the following people's
photographs appear are listed below. All other
photographs are by Craig C. Freeman.
Paul R. Roberts: 44, 58, 96, 98, 129, 141,
146, 153, 154, 160, 167, 170, 184, 210, 215,
253, 255, 256
Eileen K. Schofield: 69, 79, 82, 84 (right),
105 (right), 120, 123, 147, 177, 220
(left), 231, 237
Kansas Wildflower Society Slide Collection:
Anonymous: 19, 53
Paul W. Carter: 46, 104
Loren E. Fred: 31, 48, 171, 236, 242
Bill Piper: 67, 149, 212 (left)
Ronald L. McGregor Herbarium Slide
Collection, University of Kansas:
Ralph E. Brooks: 92, 121, 181, 187, 190, 227,
260
H. A. "Steve" Stephens: 20, 64, 86, 118, 168,
172

Contents

Preface

Two considerations guided our efforts in producing this book. First, we saw the need for an attractive, informative, and convenient field guide to the common wildflowers of the southern Great Plains. Our intent was not to write an exhaustive treatise on the region's flora. Comprehensive information can be found in the *Flora of the Great Plains* (Lawrence: University Press of Kansas, 1986) and its older companion work, *Atlas of the Flora of the Great Plains* (Ames: Iowa State University Press, 1977). Rather, we wanted to provide a handy reference that would cater to the needs of a mostly lay audience having little or no formal training in botany or plant systematics. Popular field guides and identification manuals are available for portions of the Great Plains and peripheral regions. We hope this book will complement those works.

We believe that several of this book's features will prove attractive to travelers, vacationers, and weekend botanists, as well as seasoned wildflower enthusiasts. The generous use of color photographs and line drawings, the nontechnical descriptions, and a format designed to aid with plant identifications should appeal to a large audience with diverse interests.

Our underlying concern for the environment also motivated us to write this book. Public awareness of environmental issues and interest in our natural biological heritage are at an unprecedented level, stimulating a tremendous demand for information about plants, animals, and natural communities. We hope this book will satisfy some of that demand and kindle further interest in the flora of the Great Plains. We hope, too, that it will instill a greater appreciation and understanding of the natural world.

The assistance of numerous people made this endeavor possible. First and foremost are our spouses. Jane Freeman and Ted Barkley supported our efforts, provided encouragement, and made many sacrifices so that we might realize our goal. We thank the staff of the University Press of Kansas for having faith in our ideas and confidence in our abilities. Dr. Edward Martinko, director of the Kansas Biological Survey, endorsed Craig Freeman's involvement and allowed him to devote considerable time to the project. His support is greatly appreciated. The rest of the staff of the Survey also are acknowledged for their patience. Dr. Ralph E. Brooks of the Ronald L. McGregor Herbarium, University of Kansas, and Dr. T. M. Barkley of the Kansas State University Herbarium kindly permitted us to use their facilities and loaned specimens used for the illustrations. Dr. Brooks also allowed us to use photographs from the herbarium slide collection. Sara Hall and Jane Freeman assisted with typing and organization of the manuscript. Vera Sehon expertly prepared the maps. We also thank all the wildflower enthusiasts who encouraged us, particularly the members of the Kansas Wildflower Society. We are especially indebted to Sheldon Cohen and Paul Roberts for their generous help.

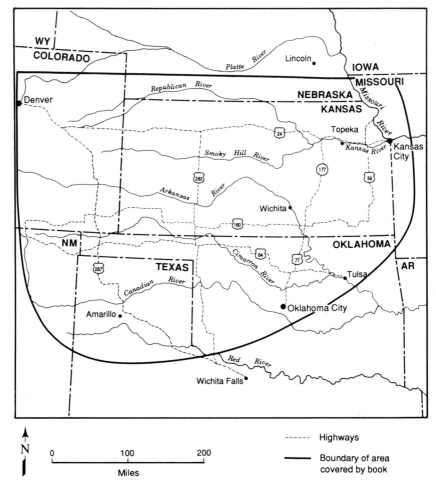

N

| 0 | 100 | 200 |

Miles

- - - - - Highways

——— Boundary of area covered by book

Figure 1. The region covered by this book.

Introduction

This book provides an introduction to roadside wildflowers of the southern Great Plains, an area that covers essentially the southern half of the geographic region included in the *Flora of the Great Plains* (Figure 1). Although somewhat vaguely defined, the area encompasses the southern edge of Nebraska, all of Kansas, much of eastern Colorado, northeastern New Mexico, the Texas Panhandle, and the northwestern half of Oklahoma.

The typical stereotype of the Great Plains is one of a flat, drab, and unchanging landscape. True, the plains do not offer lofty mountain peaks or breathtaking canyons, but they have a magnificence and allure that are unique. The beauty of the plains is often subtle, such as their virtually imperceptible ascent from the Missouri River west to the foot of the Rocky Mountains. They support a varied assemblage of plants and animals. Each of these organisms has developed its own way of coping with the changeable and often harsh environment that typifies the region.

An estimated twenty-five hundred species of vascular plants occur in the southern Great Plains. Unfortunately, most travelers and many who live in the region are unaware of the natural diversity that surrounds them. The plains can be a source of great enjoyment for those willing to take the time to stop and look, and they can offer us tantalizing glimpses into the complex natural world of which we are a part.

The Vegetation of the Southern Great Plains

The Great Plains cover an immense area of central North America. The exact limits of the region are imprecise, but this expansive east-sloping plain is situated east of the Rocky Mountain uplift and west of the eastern deciduous forests, stretching from southern Canada, south into central Texas.

Prior to European settlement, the Great Plains were dominated by vast grasslands. In less than two centuries, man has profoundly altered the character of this region. The present landscape bears little resemblance to what was once a veritable sea of grasses. A few large unspoiled tracts remain, like the Flint Hills of Kansas and Oklahoma and the Sandhills of Nebraska, but most of the original vegetation has been plowed, heavily grazed, or logged. Today, the native flora and fauna persist largely in scattered enclaves within a patchwork of agricultural and developed land.

Regional transitions in the native vegetation of the Great Plains are mostly gradual. Only in instances where there are abrupt transitions in substrate (for example, from limestone to dune sands) or in water availability do pronounced shifts occur in the character of the vegetation. Where vegetation transitions do exist, they can be striking if accentuated by blooms of wildflowers.

Three major grassland types in the southern Great Plains lie in roughly parallel north-south bands (Figure 2). The wettest of these occurs in the east. Moisture availability decreases toward the west into the rain shadow of the Rocky Mountains, and there is a gradual shift to vegetation types dominated by drought-tolerant species. Along the eastern edge of the region, the prairie forms a mosaic

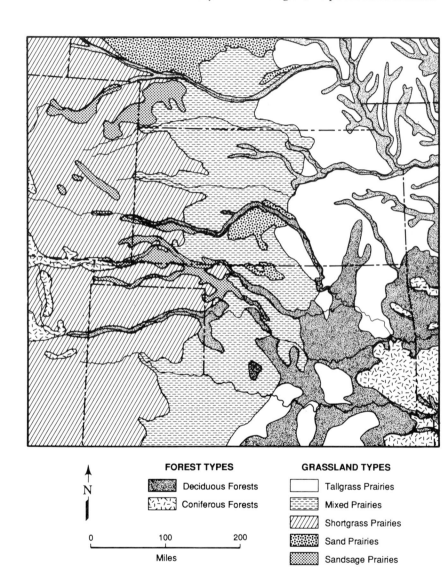

FOREST TYPES

Deciduous Forests

Coniferous Forests

N

0   100   200

Miles

GRASSLAND TYPES

Tallgrass Prairies

Mixed Prairies

Shortgrass Prairies

Sand Prairies

Sandsage Prairies

Figure 2. The distribution of major vegetation types in the southern Great Plains. Adapted from A. W. Küchler, Potential Natural Vegetation of the Conterminous United States, *American Geographical Society Special Publication 36 (New York: American Geographical Society, 1964).*

with deciduous forests. Some of these forests have ribbon-like extensions into the plains along rivers and streams where sufficient water is available to support woody species. Along the western edge of the region, the prairie gives way to coniferous forests, mostly above elevations of five thousand feet.

Tallgrass prairie is the wettest and most luxuriant of the grassland types in the Great Plains, supporting an abundance of grasses and forbs (herbs other than grasses). The western edge of the Flint Hills approximates the western limit of tallgrass prairie in the southern Great Plains. Four grass species dominate this prairie type: big bluestem (*Andropogon gerardii* Vitman), little bluestem (*A. scoparius* Michx.), Indiangrass [*Sorghastrum nutans* (L.) Nash], and switchgrass (*Panicum virgatum* L.).

Mixed prairie or mixed-grass prairie is a transitional type between tallgrass and shortgrass prairies. The vegetation is a blend of tallgrass and shortgrass species and is an expression of the interplay of these species as influenced by climate, fire, and grazing. Boundaries of the mixed prairie are defined rather poorly, but this type comprises essentially the central third of the southern Great Plains. Little bluestem and blue grama [*Bouteloua gracilis* (H.B.K.) Lag. ex Griffiths] are the dominant grasses in most areas.

Shortgrass prairie is found throughout the western third of the Great Plains where rainfall is minimal. The infamous dust bowl of the 1930s resulted from crippling droughts that affected large areas of shortgrass prairie that had been plowed for row crops. Low sod-forming grasses dominate this prairie type, including buffalo grass [*Buchloë dactyloides* (Nutt.) Engelm.] and blue grama.

Abundant tracts of sandy soil and sand dunes occur in the southern Great Plains, particularly in the western half. The most conspicuous areas are situated immediately south of the major rivers, especially the South Platte, Arkansas, and Cimarron. Sand dunes formed during the last glacial episode when fierce, northerly winds swept vast amounts of sand and silt out of sediment-choked rivers and redeposited them downwind from the river channels. Dune areas often have a rolling or hummocky appearance. In south-central Kansas and north-central Oklahoma, sand prairies are dominated by sand bluestem (*Andropogon hallii* Hack.) and sandreed (*Calamovilfa*). Farther west, they are replaced by sandsage prairie where sandsage or sand sagebrush (*Artemisia filifolia* Torr.) becomes a prominent component. The vegetation of both sand and sandsage prairies tends to be patchy, and annual forbs are abundant.

Prior to European settlement, forested areas were confined largely to the valleys and floodplains. Since then, woodlands and forests have actually increased at the expense of prairies, in part because of the suppression of fire throughout the region.

Although this book is most useful within the southern Great Plains, it has some utility in peripheral areas. Most of the wildflowers have ranges that lie partly outside our region. Range information approximates the area in which each species is most likely to be encountered. For example, a plant with a range given as "SW ¼" (southwestern quarter) can be expected in suitable habitat in southeastern Colorado, southwestern Kansas, extreme northeastern New Mexico, and the panhandles of Oklahoma and Texas. Likewise, habitat information is general, except in instances where species exhibit a high degree of habitat fidelity.

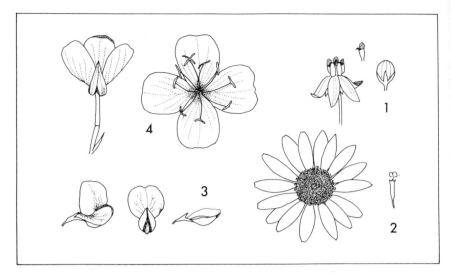

Figure 3. The flowers of four common plant families in the southern Great Plains: (1) Asclepiadaceae (Milkweed Family), (2) Asteraceae (Sunflower Family), (3) Fabaceae (Bean Family), and (4) Onagraceae (Evening Primrose Family).

Members of four plant families constitute nearly 40 percent of all species in the southern Great Plains: the Asteraceae (Sunflower Family), Poaceae (Grass Family), Cyperaceae (Sedge Family), and Fabaceae (Bean Family). Other sizable families include the Scrophulariceae (Figwort Family), Lamiaceae (Mint Family), Brassicaceae (Mustard Family), Rosaceae (Rose Family), Onagraceae (Evening Primrose Family), Euphorbiaceae (Spurge Family), and Polygonaceae (Buckwheat Family).

Nearly half of the wildflowers in this book belong to four common families: Asclepiadaceae, Asteraceae, Fabaceae, and Onagraceae. A general familiarity with some of their basic features (shown in Figure 3) will permit the beginner to recognize the family affiliation of many species.

The Milkweed Family is represented mainly by the genus *Asclepias* in this book; however, this genus includes some of our most attractive and prominent wildflowers. Most of our milkweeds have milky sap, opposite leaves, and flowers borne in umbels. Milkweed flowers are highly modified. The five sepals and five petals are often hidden by an elaborate, columnar structure composed of the modified stamens and pistil. Flowers often bear five colorful hoods frequently containing tiny hornlike projections.

The Sunflower Family is one of the largest groups of flowering plants in the world. The vegetative features of its members are highly variable, but species are distinguished by reduced flowers (florets) bunched together in an inflorescence called a head. The sepals typically are modified into bristles, barbs, or scales that may function in the dispersal of the fruits. The heads of many species consist of two types of florets: tubular or goblet-shaped disk florets in the center of the head, and strap-shaped ray florets around the periphery of the head. This arrangement often has the appearance of a single large flower, as in a sunflower. In other members, disk or ray florets make up the entire head, as in thistles and dandelions, respectively. Species in one large group that includes the dandelion and its relatives frequently contain milky sap. Fruits in this family are small seed-like achenes.

The Bean Family also is a diverse group. It includes many economically important species. Members can often be recognized by their irregularly shaped flowers, which bear a fanciful resemblance to butterflies. The lower two petals are joined to form a keel, two lateral petals are winglike, and the upper petal typically is erect and prominent. Many members of the Bean Family in this book have ten stamens—nine are fused by their filaments and one is left free. Leaves frequently are compound, and the fruit is a legume containing one to many seeds.

The Evening Primrose Family includes numerous showy ornamentals. The flowers of many species open only at dawn or dusk—hence the common name of the family. Most members have four sepals, and the four petals form a slender floral tube atop the ovary. There are usually eight stamens. Fruits in these species are slender capsules containing many small angular seeds.

The Scope of the Book

This book is a guide to two hundred thirty-nine common wildflowers found in the southern Great Plains. No precise or universal definition for wildflower exists. The term usually connotes plants with flowers that are eye-catching because of their color, shape, or size. Many plants in the region fit this definition; certainly more than could be included in this book.

Only those species distributed throughout at least one-quarter of the southern Great Plains are included, thus excluding plants with highly limited distributions within the region. The selection emphasizes herbaceous prairie plants that are visible along roadsides. True forest wildflowers are not included. Both native and introduced species are treated. Many of our wildflowers come from foreign lands but adapted to life on the plains. Some of these may be considered weeds, even though they have attractive and noticeable flowers. A few diminutive but interesting wildflowers are included to challenge the serious wildflower enthusiast.

All grasses and grasslike plants are excluded. These plants constitute a significant portion of the Great Plains flora, and they are the dominant elements of our grasslands. Unfortunately, their flowers are small, drab, and highly modified, making their identification difficult. Including them would have complicated the organization of the book, and seldom are they considered wildflowers. Finally, our choice of plants was influenced in a few cases by the availability of good photographs.

The Format of the Wildflower Treatments

Plants are arranged by flower color. Within each color class, wildflowers are ordered by flowering sequence. This arrangement was chosen to assist the user with the identification of plants. Simple keys are also included for those who wish to use them.

Descriptions follow a uniform format.

Each wildflower is described briefly, and information pertinent to its blooming period, habitat, and regional distribution is presented. Notes on economic or craft uses, derivation of names, or unusual characteristics are given for some species. Related species that grow in the area are also mentioned.

Each description is accompanied by one or more photographs. Line drawings highlight characteristics that are not shown in the photographs, but are useful in identification—for example, fruits that are noticeable along roadsides. Illustrated features are denoted by asterisks in the descriptions. Scale is not indicated on the drawings or photographs but can be estimated from measurements in the descriptions.

The Meaning of Plant Names

Scientific names are Latin words or words from other languages that have been Latinized. They can be intimidating to persons unfamiliar with them, but botanists use them because they have advantages over common names. Rules of nomenclature, established by botanists who name, describe, and study plants, are followed throughout the world. Thus, scientific names have universal meaning. They also convey information about the relationships among species.

Each scientific name contains two words. The first is the genus name; the second is the specific epithet. Both words are necessary to refer to a species, such as *Asclepias speciosa,* the showy milkweed. Closely related species, such as the butterfly milkweed (*Asclepias tuberosa*), bear the same genus name but have different specific epithets.

An authority citation follows the Latin name. This is the name or abbreviated name of the individual who first described the plant according to the rules of nomenclature. The authority citation is a part of the scientific name of plants. Thus, the full and proper name of showy milkweed is *Asclepias speciosa* Torr. This author citation is a standard abbreviation for John Torrey, an eighteenth-century physician and professor of chemistry and botany. Frequently, a name will have two authorities, with the first in parentheses, such as *Quincula lobata* (Torr.) Raf. This indicates that the first author, John Torrey, provided the specific epithet *lobata* but in a different genus (in this case, *Physalis*). Constantine Rafinesque later transferred the species to its current genus.

Many species exhibit obvious patterns of variation throughout their ranges. Distinctive phases may be given subspecies or variety names, abbreviated as "subsp." and "var.," respectively. An example is *Oenothera màcrocarpa* Nutt., which has four subspecies in the Great Plains. *Oenothera macrocarpa* subsp. *fremontii* (S. Wats.) W. L. Wagner, Fremont's evening primrose, is the name given to small-flowered plants found in north-central Kansas and south-central Nebraska.

Most wildflowers have common names as well. Unlike scientific names, their application is not regulated by formal rules, and they can cause confusion. Many plants have two or more common names, and the same common name can be applied to two unrelated plants. Some common names are the same as the genus name, such as stenosiphon, chamaesaracha, and aster. Others are English translations of the Latin name (for example, sunflower, from *Helianthus*). Still others are descriptive of the plant. The common name you use for a wildflower is a matter of personal preference, often influenced by the wildflower guide or identification manual you use. No attempt was made to provide a comprehensive list of common names, but at least one is included for each wildflower. Common names in this book are derived from *Flora of the Great Plains,* supplemented by Anderson and Owensby's *Common Names of a Selected List of Plants* (see References).

Families consist of related genera, such as *Calylophus* and *Oenothera,* members of the Onagraceae, or Evening Primrose Family. Flower features, such as the number of petals, ovary position, and number of pistils, are important in defining families. By some classifications, there are nearly four hundred families of flowering plants in the world. Approximately 40 percent of these are represented in the Great Plains. This book includes representatives of fifty-seven families. Scientific family names can be recognized by their *-aceae* ending. Common names for families also are those used in the *Flora of the Great Plains.*

The Use of Botanical Terminology

The identification of wildflowers requires a rudimentary knowledge of plant parts. Botanists employ an elaborate and precise jargon to describe plants. We have attempted to limit the number of technical terms in the descriptions and keys by using nontechnical words wherever possible. A glossary provides definitions for many of the botanical terms in the descriptions. Each description characterizes six basic elements in the following order: habit, stem, leaves, inflorescences, flowers, and fruits. Measurements are often given as ranges that encompass most of the variation in size of a structure.

Flowering Times

Flowering time can vary considerably within a species, depending on climate and location. As a general rule, southern plants flower earlier than northern plants, and plants growing at lower elevations flower earlier than their relatives at higher elevations. Some wildflowers may bloom more than once in a year if climatic conditions are suitable. This is particularly common among species that grow in dry regions (for example, the shortgrass prairie). In such environments, plant growth and flowering typically mirror precipitation patterns.

Finding and Enjoying Wildflowers

Wildflowers are ubiquitous, and you need not venture far to view them. However, they provide the perfect excuse to revisit familiar sites and to explore new ones. One of the most enjoyable aspects of studying wildflowers is that every week of the growing season brings a new mix of colors to nature's palette.

An extensive system of federal and state highways and county roads permits access to most areas of the Great Plains. Almost every wildflower enthusiast has a favored route or routes for viewing wildflowers. For the benefit of those traveling through the region and looking for alternative roads and for beginning wildflower watchers, we suggest a few routes that offer good displays of wildflowers.

Selected federal and state highways that are scenic for much of their length and provide the traveler with an excellent opportunity to study the major vegetation types of the region are shown in Figure 1. East-west routes, such as U.S. 24, U.S. 160, and U.S. 64, take the traveler from tallgrass prairie and deciduous forest in the east, through mixed prairie, to shortgrass prairie in the west. U.S. 59, mostly along its southern half, offers views of tallgrass prairie remnants used predominantly as native hay meadows. The highway also traverses many beautiful tree-lined rivers and streams. KS 177 is situated in the heart of the Kansas Flint Hills. Spring and fall typically provide outstanding tallgrass vistas along the route. U.S. 283 lies along the western edge of the mixed prairie, and the Red Hills region of Kansas and Oklahoma offers superb wildflower displays. Sandsage prairies can be seen where the highway crosses the Arkansas, Cimarron, and North Canadian rivers. U.S. 287 makes a lazy arc through the shortgrass prairie from Denver to Wichita Falls. Wildflower blooms are most spectacular following rains.

State- and federally owned lands accessible to the public provide sites where wildflowers can be observed and enjoyed. Numerous state parks and recreational areas dot the region—more than can be enumerated here. Access to these areas often requires a nominal user's fee, but our experience is that the scenery and wildflower viewing are well worth the cost. Many areas are well known and

heavily visited because of their proximity to cities, their excellent facilities, or their beauty. However, don't overlook out-of-the-way places. They can provide outstanding wildflower viewing, and you will not have to battle the crowds.

The federal government owns and manages several national wildlife refuges and national grasslands in the region that include some outstanding examples of the native flora. Five national grasslands in the southern Great Plains contain over eight hundred thousand acres of public land managed by the U.S. Forest Service. These include the Comanche in southeast Colorado, the Cimarron in southwest Kansas, the Kiowa in northeast New Mexico, the Black Kettle in Oklahoma, and the Rita Blanca in Oklahoma and Texas.

The best way to capture the beauty of wildflowers is in photographs. Flowers should not be picked unless they are abundant in an area. The dried fruits we mention for use in winter arrangements should be picked after the seeds have dispersed. Our stewardship and careful management can ensure that roadside wildflowers of the southern Great Plains will be here for future generations to enjoy.

Plant Identification

Unknown plants may be identified with this book by two means. A comparative approach may be used, wherein a specimen is compared with photographs, drawings, and descriptions to determine its identity. To aid in this process, wildflowers are arranged in four classes based on flower or inflorescence color: white, greenish white, or green; pink, red, or brown; blue, lavender, violet, or purple; and yellow or orange. Some colors in the pink to violet to blue range are difficult to photograph accurately. We have tried to describe them broadly and provide photographs that are representative of the true flower color. Some liberty has been taken to permit the grouping of related species within classes. Wildflowers are arranged roughly according to flowering sequence within each color class. Thus, for example, a plant with white flowers observed in September should be sought toward the end of the section on white-flowered species.

Identification keys are provided for those who wish to take a more direct and analytical approach. They consist of a series of paired statements, or couplets, that describe the plants. For each couplet, the user selects the statement true of the specimen in question. Following the statement chosen is a reference to the next couplet that must be evaluated or the page number of one or more species. A final determination can be made from a group of similar species by comparing the plant with photographs and descriptions.

For example, suppose you find a plant with brilliant red flowers growing along a stream in central Oklahoma. It has alternate leaves and when a leaf is plucked from the plant, milky sap emerges. You turn to Key 2: Flowers or Inflorescences Predominantly Pink, Red, or Brown. Leaves are present, so you select the second statement of couplet 1 and proceed to couplet 2. The leaves and stems lack prickles, so again you select the second statement, proceeding to couplet 5. The stem has milky sap, which agrees with the first statement of the couplet, and this takes you to couplet 6. Finally, the alternate leaves of your plant guide you to the second statement of the couplet, which provides the page numbers of two possible plants. A quick comparison of the photographs and descriptions reveals the plant to be the cardinal flower, *Lobelia cardinalis* L.

Key characters generally are attributes that are easy to examine and evaluate. In some instances, however, it may be necessary to open a flower to count stamens or make a close inspection of stems or leaves to look for certain types of hairs. A hand lens or small magnifying glass is useful in these cases. The keys in this book are designed only to permit the identification of the species illustrated herein. Thus, many Great Plains plants cannot be identified with this book. If several unsuccessful attempts are made to identify a plant, it may be necessary to consult one of the additional works cited in the References.

A few words of caution are appropriate for beginners attempting to identify plants. Flower color varies markedly in some wildflowers, whereas in others it is constant. Variation also occurs in other characteristics such as size, shape, and hairiness. This natural variation results from the complex interplay of genetic and environmental factors. It is the raw material of evolution and is desirable to plant breeders who seek to modify crop and ornamental species. However, natural variation can cause considerable distress for someone attempting to put a name on an unfamiliar wildflower. If attempts to identify a plant in one color class are unsuccessful, better luck may be found in another color class, particularly if flower color is variable. Species are placed in classes by their most frequent color, and the range of flower colors for species is given in the descriptions. However, plants with variable flower color may be found in two or more keys. Field bindweed (*Convolvulus arvensis* L.) is a good example of a plant with flowers that typically are white but sometimes are pink or pink-striped. This species can be identified in Keys 1 and 2.

Identification Keys

Key 1.
Flowers or Inflorescences Predominantly White, Greenish White, or Green.

1. Stems with milky sap . . . . 2.
   2. Stems scrambling or climbing . . . . p. 79
   2. Stems spreading to erect . . . . 3.
      3. Sap yellowish orange . . . . p. 58
      3. Sap white . . . . 4.
         4. Leaves mostly opposite or in whorls . . . . pp. 59, 66, 72, 73, 75, 87
         4. Leaves mostly alternate. . . . . pp. 39, 51, 74, 82, 83
1. Stems without milky sap . . . . 5.
   5. Stems with prickles . . . . pp. 28, 29, 55
   5. Stems without prickles . . . . 6.
      6. Leaves absent . . . . p. 92
      6. Leaves present . . . . 7.
         7. Stems twining or trailing . . . . pp. 80, 81
         7. Stems spreading to erect . . . . 8.
            8. Shrubs or small trees . . . . pp. 26, 27, 38, 65
            8. Herbs . . . . 9.
               9. Flowers in heads . . . . 10.

27. Flowers with a short to long,
slender floral tube atop the   pp. 37, 53,
ovary, and petals all alike   62, 95, 111
27. Flowers without a slender
floral tube atop the ovary,
and petals not all alike . .   p. 49
26. Stamens more or fewer than 8   28.
28. Stamens always 5 . . . .   29.
29. Inflorescence a loose to
.tightly coiled cluster of   pp. 46, 47,
flowers   86
29. Inflorescence not a   pp. 30, 54,
coiled cluster of flowers   91, 136
28. Stamens more or fewer than
5 . . . .   30.
30. Leaves bayonetlike . .   p. 43
30. Leaves not bayonetlike   31.
31. Stamens always 4   pp. 32, 52
31. Stamens more or   pp. 25, 31,
fewer than 4 . . .   84, 94, 99

Key 2.
Flowers or Inflorescences Predominantly Pink, Red, or Brown.

1. Leaves absent; plant with spines . . . . p. 118
1. Leaves present . . . . 2.
2. Leaves and stems with prickles. . . . . 3.
3. Leaves twice pinnately compound . . . . p. 112
3. Leaves entire or once compound . . . . 4.
4. Flowers in heads . . . . pp. 121,
129, 187
4. Flowers not in heads . . . . pp. 55, 120
2. Leaves and stems without prickles . . . . 5.
5. Stems with milky sap . . . . 6.
6. Leaves opposite . . . . pp. 117, 131
6. Leaves alternate . . . . pp. 140, 176
5. Stems without milky sap . . . . 7.
7. Plant onionlike . . . . p. 107
7. Plant not onionlike . . . . 8.
8. Stamens more than 10, united by their filaments into a column . . pp. 78, 104,
105, 113,
201
8. Stamens 10 or fewer, united or separate . . . . 9.
9. Stems creeping, crawling, or climbing. . . . . 10.
10. Leaves compound . . . . 11.
11. Leaves opposite . . . . pp. 168, 231
11. Leaves alternate . . . . pp. 123,
137, 144,
180

Key 3.
Flowers or Inflorescences Predominantly Blue, Lavender, Violet, or Purple.

Key 4.
*Flowers or Inflorescences Predominantly
Yellow or Orange.*

Roadside Wildflowers

of the Southern Great Plains

White, Greenish White, or Green

Townsendia exscapa (Richards.) Porter

Easter daisy

Asteraceae
Sunflower Family

Description
Easter daisy is a low, stemless, somewhat tufted, hairy, perennial herb arising from a branched rootstock and deep taproot. Leaves are basal, simple, entire, lance-shaped to narrowly lance-shaped, ½–3 in. long, and less than ¼ in. wide. Heads are sessile among the leaves and up to 1½ in. wide. Bracts on the heads are narrowly lance-shaped; ray florets are 20–40, white to pinkish, and up to ¾ in. long; disk florets are numerous and yellow, sometimes tinged pink or purple. Fruits are flattened, ribbed, hairy achenes tipped with slender white bristles.

Blooming Period
March–May.

Habitat
Mixed and shortgrass prairies, especially on dry rocky slopes; W ½.

This beautiful little composite is among the earliest flowering wildflowers on prairies in the western half of the region. It is often observed in bloom around Easter—hence its common name.

Antennaria neglecta Greene

Field pussy-toes

Asteraceae
Sunflower Family

Description
Field pussy-toes is a short, colonial, perennial herb with long stolons. Flowering stems are erect, white-woolly, and 2–12 in. tall. Leaves are mostly basal, simple, entire, stalked, spatula-shaped, 1–2½ in. long, ¼–¾ in. wide, and generally white-woolly beneath and dark green above; leaves on the flowering stems are small and often have a curled tip. Male and female flowers are produced on separate plants in heads ¼–½ in. across and in clusters of few to many near the tips of the stems; disk florets are white; ray florets are absent. Fruits are small cylindrical achenes with white bristles at the top.

Blooming Period
March–June.

Habitat
Dry to moist tallgrass prairies, open woods, and pastures; NE ½.

Male plants can be recognized by the brownish stamens projecting from the florets. Female plants bear heads that are uniformly white and slightly larger. Field pussy-toes is readily observed in the early spring in hay meadows and pastures, where the vegetation is short. The basal leaves of plants are often found among the grasses long after flowering is completed.

Astragalus racemosus Pursh

Alkali milk-vetch,
Creamy milk-vetch

Fabaceae
Bean Family

Description
Alkali milk-vetch is a coarse, sparsely to densely hairy, perennial herb with a stout woody taproot. Stems are few to many, often reddish, mostly erect, and ½–2½ ft. tall. Leaves are alternate, 2–6 in. long, ½–1 in. wide, and odd-pinnately compound, with 5–15 pairs of elliptic leaflets. Inflorescences are elongate racemes of 15–70 nodding flowers on long stalks arising from the bases of leaves. The corolla is white to pale purplish white, sometimes white with a bluish spot on the joined petals; the 10 stamens are in 2 groups, 9 joined by their filaments and 1 free. Fruits* are drooping, angular, elongate legumes containing dark brown seeds.

Blooming Period
March–July.

Habitat
Shortgrass and mixed prairies in limestone, clay, shale, and gypsum soils; W ½.

This species is toxic to livestock because it accumulates and stores selenium from the soil. When ingested, selenium interferes with protein synthesis.

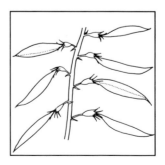

Cymopterus montanus T. & G.

Mountain corkwing,
Mountain cymopterus

Apiaceae
Parsley Family

Description
Mountain corkwing is a low, stemless, smooth, pale-green, perennial herb, rarely over 6 in. tall, arising from a thickened root. Leaves are clustered in a basal rosette, stalked, somewhat fleshy, egg-shaped to triangular in outline, pinnately lobed, ½–5 in. long, and ¼–2 in. wide. Inflorescences are compact umbels on stalks rarely longer than the leaves, bearing prominent, dry, papery, white and green bracts just below the umbels. Flowers are very small, with 5 whitish purple to greenish white petals. Fruits* are dry and egg-shaped, with 2 prominently winged segments.

Blooming Period
March–May.

Habitat
Open, rocky, mixed and shortgrass prairies; W ½.

Stemless corkwing [*C. acaulis* (Pursh) Raf.] occurs throughout the northwestern quarter of the region. It is distinguished by entirely green bracts below the umbels. Wild parsleys (*Lomatium*) resemble corkwings; however, they have inflorescences that are more open.

Nothoscordum bivalve (L.) Britt.

False garlic

Liliaceae
Lily Family

Description
False garlic is an erect, stemless, perennial herb arising from a small bulb. Plants have an onionlike appearance but lack the odor of onions. Leaves are basal, 2–6 in number, 4–12 in. long, and mostly less than ⅛ in. wide. Inflorescences are solitary terminal umbels of 3–12 flowers on naked stalks about as long as the leaves. Flowers are white with yellowish streaks or pale yellow; the 6 narrowly egg-shaped corolla lobes are similar; stamens are 6. Fruits are small, spherical, slightly 3-angled capsules containing many small, black, angular seeds.

Blooming Period
April–May, sometimes again in October.

Habitat
Tallgrass prairies, pastures, roadsides, and open woods; SE ½.

This is the only member of a genus of roughly 36 species that occurs in our region. It is occasionally mistaken for an onion (*Allium*); however, the absence of an onionlike odor, yellowish flowers, and more numerous seeds are reliable features for identification.

Sisyrinchium campestre Bickn.

White-eyed grass

Iridaceae
Iris Family

Description

White-eyed grass is an erect, waxy, pale-green, grasslike, perennial herb ¼–1½ ft. tall, with fibrous roots. Stems are tufted, flat, winged, and unbranched. Leaves are mostly basal, simple, sessile, entire, linear, 3–10 in. long, and less than ⅛ in. wide. Inflorescences are umbel-like clusters of a few flowers at the ends of stems and arising from several pointed leaflike bracts. Flowers are flattened to shallowly funnel-shaped, white to pale blue and often yellowish at the center, and with 6 similar segments less than ½ in. long; there are 3 stamens with orange anthers. Fruits are small, spherical, green to brown capsules containing many small black seeds.

Blooming Period
April–June.

Habitat
Tallgrass prairies and infrequently in open woods; E ⅓.

Blue-eyed grass (*S. angustifolium* P. Mill.) is a taller bright green plant with pale-blue to violet flowers. It is found on tallgrass and mixed prairies and in moist open woods largely in the southeastern half of our region.

Prairie iris (*Nemastylis geminiflora* Nutt.) is a beautiful tallgrass prairie inhabitant of the southeastern quarter of the region. Plants have 1–2 in.–wide blue flowers, leaves that are longer than the inflorescences, and bulbs.

Prunus angustifolia Marsh.

Chickasaw plum,
Sandhill plum

Rosaceae
Rose family

Description

Chickasaw plum is a multi-branched shrub mostly 3–7 ft. tall, infrequently up to 12 ft. tall, and often forming extensive thickets. Trunks are covered with reddish brown or grayish brown bark; twigs are red to brown, smooth, and angular. Leaves* are alternate, simple, stalked, smooth and shiny, often folded lengthwise, lance-shaped to elliptic, ¾–2½ in. long, and ½–¾ in. wide, with finely toothed margins. Inflorescences are scattered to dense clusters of 2–4 stalked flowers borne at the ends of short spur-like branches. Flowers appear before or with the leaves and are under ½ in. wide; sepals are 5 and mostly smooth; the 5 white petals are less than ¼ in. long; stamens are 20 and spreading. Fruits* are fleshy, red to orange, smooth, waxy, spherical, and up to ¾ in. in diameter and contain a single plump pitted stone.

Blooming Period
April.

Habitat
Nearly all prairie types but most common on sand prairies, as well as pastures, stream banks, and roadsides; throughout most of region but infrequent in W ⅕.

Prunus is a genus of about 200 species and is divided into 2 major groups. Plums, peaches, apricots, and almonds are included in the group recognized by the presence of a shallow to deep groove on the fruit. Pie and sweet cherries, by contrast, have essentially spherical ungrooved fruits.

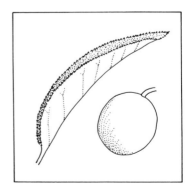

Prunus americana Marsh.

Wild plum

Rosaceae
Rose Family

Description

Wild plum is a shrub or small tree 1–3 ft. tall, that often forms thickets or colonies. The trunk is covered with grayish brown bark; twigs are orangish brown. Leaves* are alternate, simple, stalked, broadly lance-shaped to egg-shaped, 2½–4 in. long, and 1–2 in. wide, with toothed margins. Inflorescences are scattered or dense clusters of 2–5 stalked flowers borne at the ends of short spurlike branches. Flowers typically appear before the leaves and are about ¾ in. wide; sepals are 5 and hairy above; petals are 5, white, and less than ½ in. long; the 20–30 stamens are spreading. Fruits are fleshy, red to orange, smooth, somewhat

waxy, spherical, and about 1 in. in diameter and contain a single smooth compressed stone.

Blooming Period
April–May.

Habitat
Open woods, thickets, prairies, stream banks, pastures, and roadsides; throughout the region but scarce in W ¼ and apparently absent in SW ¼.

This is one of our most common plums. Fruits of native plums make a delicately flavored pink jelly. Mexican plum (*P. mexicana* S. Wats.) is similar but is usually a taller solitary tree with hairy twigs and flower stalks and purple fruits. It occurs primarily in the eastern quarter of our region.

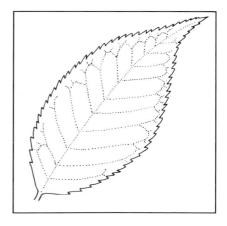

Rubus flagellaris L.

Northern dewberry

Rosaceae
Rose Family

Description
Northern dewberry is a trailing or low-arched perennial. Stems are 1½–10 ft. long, often rooted at the tips, and bearing few to many stout, slightly hooked prickles. Leaves are alternate, prickly-stalked, and compound, with 3–5 broadly lance-shaped to egg-shaped, toothed leaflets 2½–3½ in. long and 2–2½ in wide; leaflets are dark green above and slightly hairy and paler beneath. Inflorescences are flat-topped or elongate stalked clusters of few or single flowers arising from the bases of leaves; stalks of inflorescences and flowers are often glandular. Sepals are 5, densely hairy, and over ¼ in. long; petals are 5, white to pinkish, and about ½ in. long. Fruits are ½–1 in. long, black, juicy, and sweet.

Blooming Period
April–June.

Habitat
Tallgrass prairies, open woods, thickets, pastures, and roadsides; E ⅓.

Rubus includes blackberries, raspberries, and other dewberries. Most species exhibit great variation, a fact related to the ability of plants to hybridize and to reproduce by vegetative means. Six fairly distinct species are recognized in our region.

Rubus alleghaniensis Porter

Common blackberry

Rosaceae
Rose Family

Description

Common blackberry is an erect or arching perennial. Stems are 1½–10 ft. long, with a few stout, straight or hooked prickles; young stems typically are glandular. Leaves are alternate, stalked, and compound, with 3–5 egg-shaped to elliptic, toothed leaflets 2½–4 in. long and 1½–2 in. wide; leaflets are smooth and green above, slightly paler and hairy beneath. Inflorescences are elongate, cylindrical, many-flowered racemes borne near the ends of stems or arising from the bases of leaves. The sepals are 5, egg-shaped, and hairy; the petals are 5, white, and ½ in. long; stamens are nu-

merous. Fruits* are spherical, ½–¾ in. long, purplish black, juicy, and sweet.

Blooming Period
May–June.

Habitat
Tallgrass prairies, open woods, thickets, pastures, and roadsides; E ¼.

Black raspberry (*R. occidentalis* L.) is found in similar habits in the eastern third of our region. It has leaflets that are distinctly white beneath. Red raspberry [*R. idaeus* L. subsp. *sachalinensis* (Levl.) Focke] is a more northern species and does not enter our region; however, plants are found along bluffs of the Missouri River south as far as northwestern Missouri. Blackberries and raspberries are very flavorful for eating raw, as jam, or in pies.

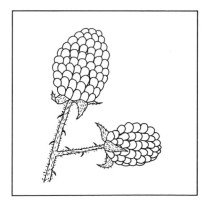

Comandra umbellata (L.) Nutt.

Bastard toadflax

Santalaceae
Sandalwood Family

Description
Bastard toadflax is a short, erect, perennial herb, often waxy and gray green, and ¼–1½ ft. tall, with an extensive system of rhizomes. Stems are clustered or single and often branched. Leaves are alternate, simple, short-stalked to sessile, entire, linear to lance-shaped or elliptic,

¼–2 in. long, and mostly less than ¼ in. wide. Inflorescences are few-flowered panicles borne near the ends of stems. The 4–5 small white or pinkish sepals are lance-shaped; petals are absent; stamens are 5. Fruits are small, rounded, and fleshy and contain a single seed.

Blooming Period
April–June.

Habitat
Dry rocky to sandy prairies and occasionally rocky open woods; scattered throughout region.

Bastard toadflax is a partial parasite, attaching to the roots of other plants and extracting water and nutrients. It is also able to produce its own food through photosynthesis.
   The Sandalwood Family includes nearly 400 species found mostly in the tropics. *Comandra* is the only member found in our region. This plant without flowers resembles toadflax (*Linaria*)— hence the common name.

Rumex venosus Pursh

Wild begonia,
Veined dock

Polygonaceae
Buckwheat Family

enlarging in fruit to ¾–1½ in. long and turning pink or reddish; there are 6 stamens. Fruits are 3-angled, light brown, ¼ in.–long achenes.

Blooming Period
April–June.

Habitat
Sand and sandsage prairies and sandy floodplains; scattered in W ⅔ and infrequent in SW ¼.

This plant is not related to cultivated begonia.

A dozen species of *Rumex* occur in the region, and all have small flowers. Several species are weedy and cause problems on cultivated and waste ground.

Description
Wild begonia is an erect or ascending perennial herb ½–1 ft. tall, with spreading rhizomes. Stems are 1 to many, sometimes branched, and often reddish. Leaves are alternate, simple, entire, thick, lance-shaped to elliptic or egg-shaped, 1–5 in. long, and ½–2 in. wide, with an obvious midvein; prominent stipules wrap around the stem at the bases of leaves. Inflorescences are inconspicuous, terminal, panicle-like clusters of tiny flowers,* becoming showy and up to 5 in. long in fruit. Sepals are 6, in 2 whorls, and small, with the inner whorl

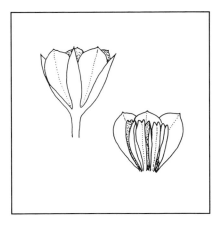

Castilleja sessiliflora Pursh

Downy paintbrush

Scrophulariaceae
Figwort Family

Blooming Period
April–June.

Habitat
Mixed and shortgrass prairies, especially on rocky slopes; W ⅔, especially in N.

Lemon paintbrush [*C. purpurea* (Nutt.) G. Don var. *citrina* (Penn.) Shinners] is common in the south-central two-thirds of the region. It has a corolla concealed by the calyx. Indian paintbrush [*C. coccinea* (L.) Spreng.] has red- or orange-colored spikes and is found on prairie hay meadows along the eastern edge of the region.

Description
Downy paintbrush is a densely soft-hairy perennial herb 4–12 in. tall. Stems are erect, mostly simple, and often clustered from a woody root. The leaves are alternate, simple, sessile, linear or the upper ones with a pair of short lobes, 1–3½ in. long, and mostly less than ¼ in. wide. Inflorescences are spikes of 10–20 flowers, each with a 1–2 in.–long green or pinkish-green bract at the base. The calyx is greenish with 5 long linear lobes; the corolla is 1½–2¼ in. long, creamy white to purplish yellow, and distinctly 2-lipped, with a prominent, arched, upper lip and a shorter lower lip with flaring lobes; the stamens are 4, in 2 groups of different lengths. Fruits* are small, woody, egg-shaped capsules bearing abundant small angular seeds.

Penstemon albidus Nutt.

White beardtongue

Scrophulariaceae
Figwort Family

glandular, and white with reddish lines within; the 5 stamens include a sterile one bearded with short yellow hairs at the tip. Fruits* are woody egg-shaped capsules containing numerous small, black, angular seeds.

Blooming Period
April–July.

Habitat
Dry mixed, shortgrass, and occasionally sandsage prairies, especially on gravelly slopes and hills; W ½.

The common name "beardtongue" is an allusion to the hairy sterile stamen (called a staminode) of many species. White beardtongue is the most common of our Great Plains penstemons.

Description
White beardtongue is an erect perennial herb ¼–2 ft. tall, with a woody rootstock. Stems are 1 to several, unbranched, short-hairy below and glandular-hairy above, especially in the inflorescence. Leaves are opposite, simple, stalked below but sessile and clasping above, entire to toothed, short-hairy, lance-shaped, 1–4 in. long, and ¼–¾ in. wide. Inflorescences are narrow, many-flowered panicles up to 11 in. long. The calyx is 5-lobed and sticky-glandular; the corolla is funnel-shaped, up to ¾ in. long, slightly 2-lipped with 2 upper lobes and 3 lower lobes, sticky-

Daucus carota L.

Queen Anne's lace,
Wild carrot

Apiaceae
Parsley Family

Description

Queen Anne's lace is an erect or spreading biennial herb 1–5 ft. tall, with a taproot. Stems are solitary, typically multi-branched, and smooth to spreading-hairy. Leaves are alternate, stalked, oblong, 2–8 in. long, 1–4 in. wide, and twice-pinnately compound, with the smallest divisions linear to lance-shaped and entire. Inflorescences are flat or rounded umbels 2–4 in. across, composed of 10–30 smaller umbellets. Flowers* are white, except for the central one of each umbellet, which is often pink or purple; there are 5 petals, sometimes unequal in size. Fruits are dry and egg-shaped, with 2 ribbed and bristly segments.

Blooming Period

April–July, not infrequently into October, especially in mowed areas.

Habitat

Tallgrass prairies, roadsides, pastures, and disturbed sites; E ⅓.

The name "Queen Anne's lace" has been traced to the wife of James I of England, who decorated her hair with the lacy leaves and flowers. The root is edible, and this species is related to the cultivated carrot.

Although often considered a weed, this graceful plant has been used in dyes and for various medicinal applications. The pressed inflorescences make delicate accents in dried-flower designs.

Hymenopappus scabiosaeus L'Her.

Old plainsman

Asteraceae
Sunflower Family

Description

Old plainsman is an erect, nearly smooth to woolly, biennial herb 1–3½ ft. tall, with a taproot. Stems are single or occasionally clustered and branched in the upper third of the plant. Leaves are alternate, stalked, 2–6 in. long, ½–3 in. wide, and once-pinnately or twice-pinnately dissected with linear segments; the basal rosette is well developed. Inflorescences are numerous clusters of heads on short stalks at the ends of branches. Bracts on the heads are whitish, especially near the tip; ray florets are absent; disk florets are numerous, funnel-shaped, creamy white, and gland-dotted. Fruits are short, hairy, black achenes with many small scales at the tip.

Blooming Period

April–July.

Habitat

Tallgrass and mixed prairies, especially on rocky limestone sites; E ½.

Old plainsman is replaced by slimleaf hymenopappus (*H. tenuifolius* Pursh) in the western half of the region, although both species occur in a narrow band through central Kansas and Oklahoma. Slimleaf hymenopappus has shorter bell-shaped disk florets and more finely dissected leaves with narrower segments. Yellow hymenopappus (*H. flavescens* A. Gray) has beautiful yellow to yellow-orange florets and occurs in the southwestern third of the region.

Abronia fragrans Nutt. ex Hook.

Sweet sand verbena

Nyctaginaceae
Four-O'Clock Family

Description
Sweet sand verbena is a low, spreading, perennial herb. Stems are 1–3 ft. long, finely hairy and sticky, frequently branched, and sometimes whitish and arise from a deep taproot. Leaves are op-posite, simple, fleshy, pale beneath, 1–5 in. long, ½–3 in. wide, and lance-shaped to triangular, with distinct stalks. Inflo-rescences are clusters of 10–40 flowers, 1–2½ in. across, at the ends of stalks that arise from the bases of the upper leaves. Flowers are fragrant, white to pinkish white, tubular, and 5-parted. Fruits are small achenes enclosed by the hard, leathery, winged calyx.

Blooming Period
April–August.

Habitat
Sandsage prairies, dunes, river and stream valleys, and disturbed sandy habi-tats; W ⅓.

Sweet sand verbena is frequently ob-served along the Arkansas, Cimarron, and Canadian rivers. Familiar horticul-tural relatives of the species include bou-gainvillea (*Bougainvillea*) and garden four-o'clock (*Mirabilis jalapa* L.).

Oenothera albicaulis Pursh

Pale evening primrose

Onagraceae
Evening Primrose Family

Description

Pale evening primrose is a short, erect, annual herb ¼–1½ ft. tall and covered with a mixture of short dense hairs and stiff spreading hairs. Stems are single, sometimes branched above, and whitish and arise from a taproot. Leaves are alternate, simple to pinnately lobed, short-stalked to sessile, spatula-shaped to lance-shaped, 1–3 in. long, and ¼–1 in. wide, with entire to wavy margins; basal leaves are usually absent on flowering plants. Flowers are single, arising from the bases of upper leaves, and have a faint unpleasant odor; buds are nodding. Sepals are 4 and reflexed; petals are 4, white or fading pale pink, ½–1½ in. long and nearly as wide, notched at the tip, and borne at the end of a slender floral tube; stamens are 8. Fruits* are ses-

sile, cylindrical, ribbed, hairy capsules containing numerous small, brownish, pitted seeds.

Blooming Period
April–August.

Habitat
Shortgrass and sandsage prairies, stream valleys, roadsides, and disturbed sites, especially in sandy soil; scattered over W ½.

Oenothera latifolia (Rydb.) Munz, also called pale evening primrose, is a white-flowered perennial often found on sand dunes and in stream valleys in the western half of the region.

Ceanothus herbaceous Raf. var. *pubescens* (T. & G.) Shinners

New Jersey tea

Rhamnaceae
Buckthorn Family

Description
New Jersey tea is a multi-branched shrub that grows up to 3 ft. tall. Stems are single or clustered, with thin grayish-brown bark; the twigs are densely hairy. Leaves are alternate, simple, stalked, egg-shaped to elliptic, 1½–2½ in. long, and ½–1 in. wide, with small teeth along the margins; the upper surface is usually dark green and smooth to hairy; the lower surface is lighter in color and moderately to densely hairy. Inflorescences are open to compact, rounded panicles produced at the ends of leafy stems. Flowers are small, white, and 5-parted. Fruits* are small, black, 3-lobed capsules containing 3 reddish brown seeds.

Blooming Period
April–August.

Habitat
Tallgrass, mixed, and shortgrass prairies, open wooded slopes, and roadsides, especially in rocky soil; E ⅔ and infrequent in S part of W ⅓.

In New Jersey during the American Revolution, the leaves of this plant were used to make tea.

Ceanothus americanus L. var. *pitcheri* T. & G., also called New Jersey tea, is common on tallgrass prairies and in open woods in the eastern third of the region. The two species are easily confused; however, *C. americanus* typically has broader leaves, inflorescences on long leafless stalks arising from the bases of leaves, and fruits with raised ridges.

Asclepias viridis Walt.

Spider milkweed,
Green antelopehorn

Asclepiadaceae
Milkweed Family

Description
Spider milkweed is a low perennial herb
1–2 ft. tall. Stems are usually solitary and
smooth and contain milky sap. Leaves
are alternate, simple, fleshy, 2–5 in. long,
½-2 in. wide, and lance-shaped to egg-
shaped. Inflorescences are umbels 3–5
in. across that contain 3–18 flowers and
are situated near the ends of stems.
Flowers are 5-parted, with greenish sepals, creamy green to pale green petals,
and red to purple hoods and no horns.
Fruits* are pods 3–6 in. long containing
abundant seeds,* each tipped with a tuft
of long white hairs.

Blooming Period
April–August.

Habitat
Sandy or rocky limestone tallgrass or
mixed prairies; E ½.

A similar species, spider antelopehorn
[*A. asperula* (Dcne.) Woods.], is found
throughout central Kansas and the
southern half of the region.
  Milkweeds possess an intriguing pollination system in which pollen is pack-
aged in small structures resembling pairs
of saddlebags. Successful pollination in-
volves an insect picking up a pair of
saddlebags from one flower and properly
placing it into a groove in another flower.

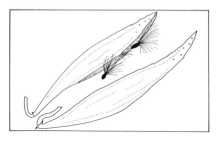

Nasturtium officinale R. Br.

Watercress

Brassicaceae
Mustard Family

Description
Watercress is a floating or creeping, smooth, somewhat fleshy, bright-green, aquatic perennial that roots at the nodes. Stems are branched and up to 3 ft. long. Leaves are alternate, stalked, pinnately compound, with 3–11 lance-shaped to egg-shaped entire leaflets; the terminal leaflet typically is larger than the lateral ones, ¼–2½ in. long, and less than 1 in. wide. Inflorescences are short racemes of white flowers. The calyx and corolla are 4-parted; there are 4 long and 2 short stamens. Fruits* are ½ in.–long, slender, upward-curved capsules; seeds are small, numerous, and brownish.

Blooming Period
April–October.

Habitat
Still and slowly flowing shallow water in and along streams, rivers, ponds, and springs; scattered throughout region but less common in W.

Watercress has long been used as a potherb, and myriad medicinal qualities have been ascribed to the plant. The species name, "*officinale*," means "used in medicine."

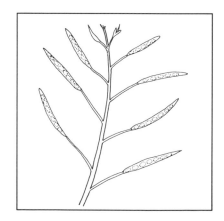

Leucelene ericoides (Torr.) Greene

White aster

Asteraceae
Sunflower Family

Description
White aster is a low, erect, hairy, perennial herb 2–6 in. tall, arising from a creeping, branched, woody rootstock. Stems are usually numerous and branched. Leaves are alternate, simple, sessile, linear, mostly less than ½ in. long, and ⅛ in. wide, with entire hairy margins. Inflorescences are solitary ½ in.–wide heads borne at the ends of branches. Ray florets are white or pinkish white and less than ¼ in. long; disk florets are yellow. Fruits are small hairy achenes, with a tuft of bristles at the tip.

Blooming Period
May–June, often again in August–September.

Habitat
Dry, open, often rocky, mixed and short-grass prairies; W ½.

Except for a few morphological differences and its habit of flowering in the spring, this species looks very much like an aster. Some botanists treated it as such in the past. It is the only member of the genus *Leucelene*.

Delphinium virescens Nutt.

Plains larkspur

Ranunculaceae
Buttercup Family

Blooming Period
May–June.

Habitat
All prairie types, pastures, and roadsides; throughout region.

This attractive plant is highly conspicuous in flower. Plants vary considerably in hairiness, flower color, and leaf shape.

Dwarf larkspur (*D. tricorne* Michx.) is a native blue-flowered perennial found primarily in woodlands in the eastern quarter of the region. Rocket larkspur (*D. ajacis* L.) is a blue-flowered annual found in the eastern two-thirds of the region. It was introduced from Europe as a garden ornamental and occasionally escapes and persists.

Description
Plains larkspur is an erect perennial herb 1–4 ft. tall, with fibrous roots. Stems are 1 to several, branched or unbranched, and soft-hairy, often with glandular hairs. Leaves are alternate, crowded, and stalked below but gradually reduced up the stem and becoming sessile, palmately divided with linear segments, 1–3 in. long, and ½–1 in. wide. Inflorescences are showy spikelike racemes of 5–50 irregular flowers. The calyx is 5-parted, the sepals petal-like, white or sometimes tinged blue, the uppermost one bearing a long curved spur; petals are 4, white, the lower two bearded; stamens are numerous. Fruits* are erect ¾ in.–long pods borne in groups of 3 and contain many small, brown, ridged seeds.

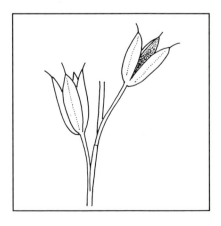

Yucca glauca Nutt.

Small soapweed

Agavaceae
Agave Family

Description
Small soapweed is a stemless semiwoody perennial that may attain a height of 3–6 ft. when in flower. Leaves are abundant, waxy green, linear, 1–3 ft. long, ¼–½ in. wide, and bayonetlike, radiating out from a stout woody rootstock. Inflorescences are elongate racemes bearing numerous drooping, creamy or greenish white, bell-shaped flowers. The 3 sepals and 3 petals are similar in shape and texture; there are 6 large stamens. Fruits* are large woody capsules containing many flat coal-black seeds.*

Blooming Period
May–July.

Habitat
Dry, often rocky prairies but much less common on tallgrass prairies, occasionally in open coniferous woodlands; throughout region.

Small soapweed is so named because the roots yield lather when pulverized and rubbed in water. Leaf fibers were used to make rope, nets, and mats. In addition, the flowers are edible.

Pollination of the species requires the small yucca moth, which collects pollen from a flower, flies to another flower, and deposits the pollen on the stigma. The moth then lays its eggs in the ovary, where the grubs feed on the developing seeds. In this well-balanced relationship, sufficient seeds remain to ensure the survival of the yucca.

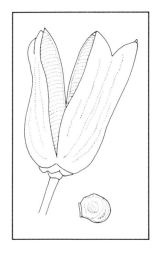

Sophora nuttalliana B. L. Turner

White loco,
Nuttall's sophora

Fabaceae
Bean Family

and up to ½ in. long; petals are white to yellowish white, and the upper petal is prominent; there are 10 separate stamens. Fruits* are beaked 1–3 in.–long legumes, usually constricted between the 1–7 smooth brownish seeds.

Blooming Period
May–July.

Habitat
Mixed, shortgrass, and sandsage prairies; W ⅔.

White loco may be mistaken for a milk-vetch (*Astragalus*); however, it is readily distinguished by its 10 separate stamens. In milk-vetches, 9 stamens are joined by their filaments and 1 is free.

Description
White loco is an erect, silky, perennial herb ¼–2 ft. tall that often forms extensive colonies by means of creeping rhizomes. Stems are 1 to many and often multi-branched from the base. Leaves are alternate, short-stalked, 1–3½ in. long, ¼–1 in. wide, and odd-pinnately compound, with 15–31, ¼–½ in.–long, entire, elliptic leaflets. Inflorescences are open to dense racemes 1½–4 in. long, arising from the bases of leaves near the ends of branches. Flowers are 5-parted

Penstemon tubaeflorus Nutt.

Tube beardtongue,
Tube penstemon

Scrophulariaceae
Figwort Family

Description
Tube beardtongue is an erect perennial herb 1–3 ft. tall, with a short woody rootstock. Stems are 1 or few, smooth, and unbranched. Leaves are opposite, simple, stalked below but sessile and clasping above, entire to slightly toothed, smooth, spatula-shaped below to lance-shaped above, 1–4 in. long, and ½–1½ in. wide. Inflorescences are narrow interrupted panicles up to 15 in. long. The calyx is 5-lobed and glandular-hairy; the corolla is funnel-shaped, up to ¾ in. long, slightly 2-lipped, with 2 upper lobes and 3 lower lobes, sticky-pubescent, and white, lacking lines

within; the 5 stamens include a yellow-bearded sterile one. Fruits* are woody egg-shaped capsules containing many small brown seeds.

Blooming Period
May–July.

Habitat
Tallgrass prairies, ditches, roadsides, open woodlands, and disturbed sites; E ½ but most abundant in E ¼.

Tube beardtongue is frequently observed in prairie hay meadows in eastern Kansas and Oklahoma. Smooth beardtongue (*P. digitalis* Nutt. ex Sims) occupies similar habitats, and the two species may be confused at first glance. However, smooth beardtongue has an open-branched inflorescence and flowers with reddish lines within.

Onosmodium molle Michx.

False gromwell

Boraginaceae
Borage Family

several to many and branched. Leaves are alternate, simple, entire, sessile, lance-shaped to egg-shaped, 2–5 in. long, and ½–2 in. wide, with 5–7 prominent nerves; basal leaves usually are absent on flowering plants. Inflorescences are terminal slightly coiled clusters that elongate in fruit. Flowers are sessile; the calyx is 5-lobed; the corolla is 5-lobed, tubular, up to ½ in long, and whitish or with erect greenish lobes; stamens are 5. Fruits are composed of 1–4 egg-shaped, smooth or pitted, whitish, stonelike nutlets, each containing a single seed.

Blooming Period
May–July.

Habitat
Dry tallgrass, mixed, sand, and infrequently shortgrass prairies, pastures, and open woods, often in sandy or gravelly soil; NE ½ and widely scattered in SW.

Description
False gromwell is an erect, coarse, stiff-hairy, grayish, perennial herb 1½–4 ft. tall, with a woody rootstock. Stems are

Cryptantha minima Rydb.

Little cryptantha

Boraginaceae
Borage Family

Description

Little cryptantha is a short, stiff-hairy, annual herb 2–6 in. tall, arising from a slender taproot. Stems are single but multi-branched from the base, with numerous erect or spreading branches. Leaves are alternate, simple, sessile, linear to spatula-shaped, ¼–1 in. long, less than ¼ in. wide, with entire margins. Inflorescences are 1–5 in. long loosely to tightly coiled clusters of flowers borne on 1 side at ends of branches. The calyx is 5-parted; the corolla is inconspicuous, white, and 5-parted; there are 5 stamens. Fruits are composed of 4 tiny bumpy nutlets, each containing a single seed.

Blooming Period

May–July.

Habitat

Dry, sandy to gravelly, mixed, shortgrass, and sandsage prairies; W ½.

Thicksepal cryptantha [*C. crassisepala* (T. & G.) Greene] is often confused with this species; however, it lacks short leafy bracts at the bases of the flowers that are on little cryptantha. Thicksepal cryptantha occurs in the western quarter of the region, often in dense patches on sandsage prairie. Bow-nut cryptantha [*C. cinerea* (Greene) Cronq. var. *jamesii* Cronq.] is a perennial species with white ¼ in.–wide flowers that is found in the western half of the region.

Conium maculatum L.

Poison hemlock

Apiaceae
Parsley Family

are small, white, and 5-parted. Fruits are egg-shaped and dry, with 2 small, prominently ribbed segments.

Blooming Period
May–July.

Habitat
Disturbed sites, including fields, pastures, thickets, roadsides, stream and river banks, and waste areas; NE ½.

This highly poisonous species was introduced from Europe. It is occasionally confused with common water hemlock (*Cicuta maculata* L.) or Queen Anne's lace (*Daucus carota* L.) but may be distinguished from the former by its more dissected fernlike leaves and from the latter by the absence of hairs and its more open inflorescences.

Description
Poison hemlock is a slender to stout erect biennial 3–10 ft. tall, arising from a stout taproot. Stems typically are branched, smooth, waxy, and purple-spotted. Leaves* are alternate, stalked, broadly triangular in outline, 3–4 times pinnately compound, with the smallest divisions coarsely toothed, and sometimes over 1 ft. long. Inflorescences are flat or rounded compound umbels 2–5 in. wide; the smaller umbels are on long and ascending or spreading stalks. Flowers

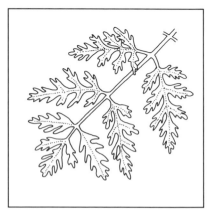

Polygala alba Nutt.

White milkwort

Polygalaceae
Milkwort Family

Description

White milkwort is an erect, smooth, perennial herb ¼–1½ ft. tall, with a stout woody taproot. Stems usually are several to many, unbranched, slightly angular, and slender. Leaves are alternate, simple, entire, sessile, narrowly lance-shaped be-low to linear above, ¼–¾ in. long, and less than ⅛ in. wide. Inflorescences are terminal racemes 1–3 in. long on slender stalks. Flowers are white with a green center and about ⅛ in. long; stamens usually are 8. Fruits are small capsules containing 2 dark hairy seeds.

Blooming Period
May–August.

Habitat
Mixed and shortgrass prairies and rarely on tallgrass prairies, especially on dry, rocky, eroded ground; W ½.

Many believed that this plant increased human lactation.

Two annual species with pink or purple flowers are found on tallgrass prairies in the eastern quarter of the region. Slender milkwort (*P. incarnata* L.) is wiry-stemmed and waxy and has a few leaves and flowers about ¼ in. long. Blood milkwort (*P. sanguinea* L.) has numerous leaves and rounded or cylindrical inflorescences with colored sepals concealing the corolla.

Polygala verticillata L.

Whorled milkwort

Polygalaceae
Milkwort Family

with a slender taproot. Stems are single, branched, and very slender. Leaves are in whorls, 2–5 per node, simple, entire, narrowly elliptic to linear, ¼–1 in. long, and less than ⅛ in. wide. Inflorescences are short, terminal, cone-shaped racemes up to 1 in. long on long slender stalks. Flowers are white or greenish pink and about ¹⁄₁₆ in. long; stamens usually are 8. Fruits are tiny capsules containing 2 black short-hairy seeds.

Blooming Period
May–October.

Habitat
Tallgrass, mixed, and sand prairies, open woods, and open disturbed sites; E ⅔.

This diminutive plant can be exceedingly difficult to find in tall, dense vegetation. The seeds of many milkworts bear small oily bodies that are gathered by ants, thus assisting in the dispersal of seeds.

Description
Whorled milkwort is an erect, smooth, inconspicuous, annual herb 2–8 in. tall,

Stillingia sylvatica L.

Queen's delight

Euphorbiaceae
Spurge Family

and a stout woody rootstock. Stems usually are several to many and unbranched. Leaves are alternate, simple, short-stalked, lance-shaped to elliptic, 1½–5 in. long, and ¼–1 in. wide, with toothed margins bearing small glands. Inflorescences are terminal and spikelike, with female flowers below the male flowers. Flowers have a small cuplike calyx and no petals; stamens are 2 in male flowers. Fruits are rounded, smooth, shallowly 3-lobed capsules about ½ in. wide, containing 3 smooth, whitish, oblong seeds.

Blooming Period
May–August.

Habitat
Sand and sandsage prairies, stream banks, roadsides, and disturbed sites; S ½.

Description
Queen's delight is an erect, smooth, perennial herb 1–3 ft. tall, with milky sap

Plantago patagonica Jacq.

Patagonian plantain

Plantaginaceae
Plantain Family

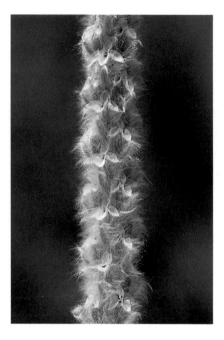

Description

Patagonian plantain is a short, stemless or nearly so, woolly, grayish, annual or biennial herb, with a slender taproot. Stems, when present, are less than 2 in. tall. Leaves are basal, simple, sessile, en-tire, linear to narrowly lance-shaped, 2–7 in. long, and less than ¼ in. wide. Inflorescences are 1 to many, 1–6 in.–long, dense, cylindrical spikes on slender naked stalks 1–10 in. long. Flowers are tiny and 4-lobed, each with a short, lance-shaped, woolly bract; the corolla is whitish or translucent, with spreading lobes; there are 4 stamens. Fruits are egg-shaped capsules about ⅛ in. long and contain 2 reddish-brown seeds.

Blooming Period
May–August.

Habitat
All prairie types, pastures, roadsides, and waste areas; throughout region.

Three varieties of this highly variable species occur in the region. They differ primarily in size and shape of the inflorescence.

Ten species of plantain are found in the southern Great Plains. All have small flowers and several are common lawn weeds.

Oenothera speciosa Nutt.

Showy evening primrose

Onagraceae
Evening Primrose Family

Description
Showy evening primrose is a short-hairy perennial herb ¾–2 ft. tall, arising from a slender rhizome. Stems are several to many and sometimes branched. Leaves are alternate, simple, short-stalked to sessile, lance-shaped to narrowly elliptic, 1–4 in. long, and ¼–1 in. wide, with shallowly toothed to deeply lobed margins. Flowers are solitary, arising from the bases of upper leaves, and showy; sepals are 4 and reflexed; petals are 4, white or pink, fading dark pink, 1–1½ in. long, at the end of a ½–1 in.–long floral tube; stamens are 8. Fruits* are elongate club-shaped capsules up to ½ in. long and contain many small brown seeds.

Blooming Period
May–August.

Habitat
Open, rocky tallgrass and mixed prairies, roadsides, and disturbed sites; E ½.

Chamaesaracha coniodes (Moric. ex Dun.) Britt.

Chamaesaracha

Solanaceae
Nightshade Family

Description

Chamaesaracha is a low, spreading, perennial herb. Stems are 2–16 in. long and covered with abundant hairs, some of them sticky. Leaves are alternate, simple, short-stalked, narrowly to broadly lance-shaped, 1–2½ in. long, and ¼–1 in. wide, often with toothed margins. Flowers are solitary or in small groups arising from the bases of leaves, ¼–½ in. across, and varying in color from white or yellowish green to pale purple; the calyx and corolla are 5-lobed; there are 5 small stamens. Fruits are many-seeded berries enclosed by the enlarged calyx.

Blooming Period

May–September.

Habitat

Sandy to gravelly shortgrass and mixed prairies, pastures, and disturbed habitats; SW ½.

Despite its diminutive size, this plant's flowers are quite attractive and well worth the extra effort often required to locate them.

Solanum carolinense L.

Carolina horse-nettle

Solanaceae
Nightshade Family

Description
Carolina horse-nettle is an erect perennial herb covered with tiny star-shaped
hairs* and short yellowish prickles.
Stems are 1–3 ft. tall and branched, arising from creeping rhizomes. Leaves are
alternate, simple, short-stalked, egg-
shaped to elliptic, the larger ones bearing
prickles along the main vein, 3–6 in.
long, 2–3 in. wide, and shallowly lobed.
Inflorescences are short racemelike clusters of 5–20 flowers. The calyx is 5-
lobed; the corolla is 5-angled, flattened,
and white to pale pink or pale violet;
there are 5 prominent yellow stamens.
Fruits are spherical yellow berries containing numerous yellowish seeds.

Blooming Period
May–September.

Habitat
Disturbed sandy to gravelly soils on tallgrass and mixed prairies and in fields,
pastures, and open woods; E ½.

The wrinkled, nearly translucent fruits of
this species are frequently seen still attached to the plant in the fall and winter.
   This large genus includes food plants
such as the Irish potato (S. tuberosum L.)
and eggplant (S. melongena L.) and well-
known poisonous plants such as black
nightshade (S. ptycanthum Dun. ex DC.).

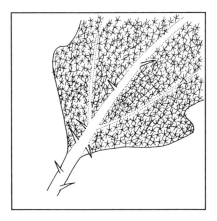

Melampodium leucanthum T. & G.

Black-foot daisy

Asteraceae
Sunflower Family

Description
Black-foot daisy is a spreading to erect, hairy, gland-dotted, perennial herb ½–1½ ft. tall, with a thick, woody, branched rootstock. Stems typically are many and branched. Leaves are opposite, simple, sessile, narrowly lance-shaped to narrowly elliptic, 1–2 in. long, and up to ½ in. wide, with entire to scarcely toothed or pinnately lobed margins. Heads are solitary, up to 1 in. wide, and on stalks up to 3 in. long, arising from the bases of upper leaves. Bracts on the heads are rounded at the tip; ray florets, which number 8–13, are creamy white, broad, and up to ½ in. long; disk florets are numerous and yellow. Fruits are short, somewhat bumpy achenes without bristles or scales.

Blooming Period
May–September.

Habitat
Open, dry shortgrass prairies, especially in limestone soil; SW ¼.

This beautiful composite is often observed with the Rocky Mountain zinnia (*Zinnia grandiflora* Nutt.) and Hartweg's evening primrose [*Calylophus hartwegii* (Benth.) Raven]. When all three are in bloom, they produce a spectacular carpet of wildflowers.

Dalea candida Michx. ex Willd.

White prairie-clover

Fabaceae
Bean Family

Description
White prairie-clover is an erect or spreading, smooth, perennial herb 1–3 ft. tall, with a woody root. Stems are 1 to several, ribbed, and sometimes branched above. Leaves are alternate, short-stalked, ½–2½ in. long, ½–1 in. wide, and odd-pinnately compound, with 3–13 elliptic to lance-shaped leaflets, with lower surfaces covered with minute glands. Inflorescences are compact, densely flowered, spherical to cylindrical spikes borne at the ends of stems. The small flowers are white, with 5 stamens joined by their filaments. Fruits are small glandular legumes containing a single seed.

Blooming Period
May–September.

Habitat
All prairie types, open woods, roadsides, and disturbed sites; throughout region.

Plants in the eastern half of our region tend to have longer unbranched stems, larger leaves, and denser inflorescences than plants in the western portion. White prairie-clover is a common legume on our prairies and readily grazed by livestock. Overgrazing can result in elimination of the species.

Argemone polyanthemos (Fedde) G. Ownbey

Prickly poppy

Papaveraceae
Poppy Family

of the flower. Fruits* are spiny egg-shaped capsules containing numerous small brownish seeds.

Blooming Period
May–September.

Habitat
Tallgrass, mixed, shortgrass, and sandsage prairies, especially in sandy soil along floodplains, roadsides, and disturbed sites; W ⅔.

Hedgehog prickly poppy (*A. squarrosa* Greene) is common in the western half of the region. It is both spiny and hairy.

The Poppy Family also includes the familiar woodland species bloodroot (*Sanguinaria canadensis* L.), which has red-orange sap.

Description
Prickly poppy is a stout, erect, annual herb with copious yellow-orange sap; a waxy coating gives the plant a bluish-green color. Stems are mostly solitary from a taproot, unbranched to branched above, spiny, and 1½–5 ft. tall. Leaves are alternate and firm; the lower ones are deeply lobed and spiny-toothed. The showy flowers are 2–4 in. across, solitary or in few-flowered groups near the ends of stems; the sepals are 3; the 6 white petals are thin, papery, and wrinkled; the stamens are abundant and bright yellow, forming a prominent sphere in the center

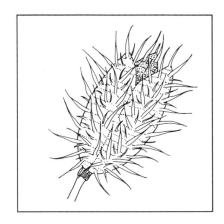

Apocynum cannabinum L.

Indian hemp dogbane, Prairie dogbane

Apocynaceae
Dogbane Family

Description
Indian hemp dogbane is a smooth to hairy perennial herb ½–3½ ft. tall, with milky sap; it frequently forms loose colonies. Stems are erect, often waxy, and branched above, arising from a creeping rhizome. Leaves are opposite, simple, sessile or short-stalked, often pale beneath, egg-shaped to lance-shaped, ½–6 in. long, and ¼–2½ in. wide. Inflorescences are dense terminal clusters. The erect or drooping greenish white to white flowers have 5 short lance-shaped calyx lobes; the bell- or urn-shaped corolla consists of 5 united petals. Fruits* are long, slender, tapering, cylindrical pods occurring in pairs and containing abundant seeds,* each with a tuft of long white or tan hairs at the tip.

Blooming Period
May–September.

Habitat
All prairie types, fields and pastures, woods, wet habitats along rivers, streams, and ponds, and disturbed sites; throughout region.

This highly variable plant has been treated as two species by botanists in the past. Fine fibers in the stems were used by Indian tribes to make rope, nets, and fabric. The Potawatomie used individual fibers to sew beads into garments.

Oleander (*Nerium oleander* L.) and lesser periwinkle (*Vinca minor* L.) are commonly cultivated members of the same family. The latter species occasionally escapes from cultivation and persists, especially in wooded areas in our region.

Melilotus alba Medic.

White sweet clover

Fabaceae
Bean Family

5-parted; there are 10 stamens, 9 joined by their filaments and 1 free. Fruits are small, smooth, brown, egg-shaped legumes containing a single seed.

Blooming Period
May–October.

Habitat
Disturbed sites, including roadsides, fields, and waste areas; throughout region.

Introduced from Eurasia, white sweet clover and its close relative, yellow sweet clover [*M. officinalis* (L.) Pall.], often grow together. Despite their weedy tendencies, both species are valued as sources of honey, for forage, and as soil stabilizers.

Description
White sweet clover is an erect, smooth to sparsely hairy, annual or biennial herb 1–7 ft. tall, with a long taproot. Stems are slender and branched. Leaves* are alternate and stalked, with 3 lance-shaped to narrowly elliptic leaflets ½–1½ in. long, less than ½ in. wide, and toothed along the margins. Inflorescences are loose, slender, 2–6 in.–long racemes on short stalks arising from the bases of leaves, mostly toward the ends of branches. Flowers are white, about ⅛ in. long, and

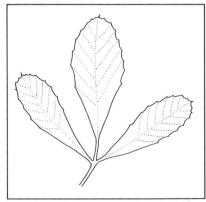

Trifolium repens L.

White clover,
Ladino clover

Fabaceae
Bean Family

rarely tinged pale pink; there are 10 stamens, 9 joined by their filaments and 1 free. Fruits are short legumes containing 2–4 yellowish seeds.

Blooming Period
May–October.

Habitat
Disturbed sites, including lawns, pastures, fields, roadsides, and waste areas; throughout the region except SW ¼.

Four-parted leaves, which are signs of good luck, occur occasionally in this species.

Description
White clover is a creeping, mat-forming, perennial herb, with a taproot. Stems* are smooth to sparingly hairy and ¼–1½ ft. long and root at the nodes. Leaves are alternate, long-stalked, and palmately compound, with 3 egg-shaped to heart-shaped finely toothed leaflets ½–1½ in. long and ¼–¾ in. wide. Inflorescences are dense rounded heads on naked stalks 2–8 in. long, arising from the bases of leaves. Flowers are 40–90, 5-parted, and less than ½ in. long; the petals are white,

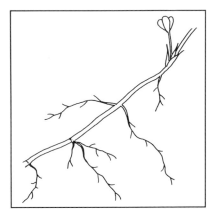

Stenosiphon linifolius (Nutt.) Heynh.

Stenosiphon

Onagraceae
Evening Primrose Family

are alternate, simple, sessile, narrowly lance-shaped to egg-shaped, ½–2 in. long, and mostly less than ½ in. wide, with entire margins; basal and lower stem leaves are usually absent at flowering. Inflorescences are short-hairy, willowy, terminal spikes. Flowers are dainty; sepals are 4, reflexed, and whitish; petals are 4, white, less than ¼ in. long, and at the end of a threadlike floral tube; stamens are 8. Fruits are short, hairy, nutlike capsules containing a single pale seed.

Blooming Period
May–October.

Habitat
All prairie types, bluffs, stream valleys, roadsides, and often on limestone; throughout region but less common in W ¼.

Description
Stenosiphon is an erect, smooth, somewhat waxy, biennial or short-lived perennial, with a woody taproot. Stems are 1 or rarely several, slender, and unbranched below the inflorescence. Leaves

Stenosiphon may be mistaken for a gaura; however, the threadlike floral tube and single seed are reliable characters for identification. It is the only member of the genus.

Polunisia dodecandra (L.) DC.

Clammy-weed

Capparaceae
Caper Family

1–3 in. long and contain numerous small reddish brown seeds.

Blooming Period
May–October.

Habitat
A variety of prairie types and disturbed sites along roadsides, pastures and fields, and waste areas, generally in sandy to gravelly soil; throughout region.

Cristatella [*P. jamesii* (T. & G.) Iltis] is a diminutive plant with unequal fringed petals. It is found in sandy habitats in the western two-thirds of the region, frequently in the exposed sand of dunes.

Description
Clammy-weed is an erect, sticky-pubescent, annual herb ½–3 ft. tall. Stems are mostly single and branched. Leaves are alternate, stalked, palmately compound with 3 lance-shaped entire leaflets 1–2 in. long and up to ½ in. wide. Inflorescences are short racemes borne at the ends of branches. Sepals are 4; petals are 4, about ½ in. long, spatula-shaped with narrow bases, and white with a tinge of pink or purple; the 10–20 stamens have slender pink or purple filaments much longer than the petals. Fruits* are cylindrical capsules

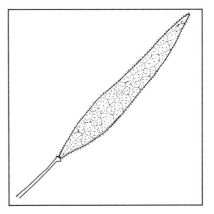

Ipomopsis longiflora (Torr.) V. Grant

White flower ipomopsis

Polemoniaceae
Phlox Family

Description

White flower ipomopsis is an erect, slender, smooth, annual or biennial herb ½–2 ft. tall. Stems are single, spreading-branched in the upper half of the plant, and occasionally glandular. Leaves are alternate, short-stalked to sessile, ½–2 in. long, and pinnately divided with 3–7 linear segments; upper leaves are entire and linear. Inflorescences are open, few-flowered to many-flowered, and panicle-like, with the flowers borne near the ends of branches. The calyx is 5-lobed; the corolla is 5-lobed, white to bluish violet, trumpet-shaped, and up to 2 in. long; stamens are 5. Fruits are small, thin, smooth capsules containing numerous small angular seeds.

Blooming Period

May–October.

Habitat

Open, dry, mixed, shortgrass, and sand-sage prairies, especially in sandy soil; W ½.

Hedyotis nigricans (Lam.) Fosb

Narrowleaf bluets

Rubiaceae
Madder Family

Description

Narrowleaf bluets is a low, erect or ascending, mostly smooth, perennial herb or subshrub ¼–1½ ft. tall, with a stout, woody, branched base. Stems are few to many and usually branched. Leaves are opposite, simple, sessile, 1-nerved, mostly linear, ¼–1½ in. long, and less than ⅛ in. wide, with entire margins. Inflorescences are crowded terminal clusters. Flowers are short-stalked or sessile; the calyx is 4-lobed; the corolla is 4-lobed, funnel-shaped, white to pink or sometimes bluish, and densely hairy within and on the lobes; stamens are 4, with blue anthers. Fruits are small egg-shaped capsules containing small black seeds.

Blooming Period

May–October.

Habitat

Nearly all prairies types, especially on dry, rocky, limestone slopes, and also along roadsides and stream valleys and in open woods; throughout region but less common in far W.

Small bluets (*H. crassifolia* Raf.) is a short, delicate, annual herb with slender stems, small spatula-shaped leaves, and tiny blue to pinkish flowers, often with a reddish throat. It occurs in short vegetation throughout the eastern third of the region.

Euphorbia dentata Michx.

Toothed spurge

Euphorbiaceae
Spurge Family

Description
Toothed spurge is an erect or spreading, somewhat hairy, annual herb ¼–2 ft. tall, with milky sap, arising from a slender taproot. Stems are single and branched. Leaves are mostly opposite, simple, stalked, narrowly lance-shaped to egg-shaped, ½–3 in. long, ¼–1½ in. wide, with toothed margins. Inflorescences are small cups borne in terminal clusters, each containing many tiny male flowers (single stamens) and a single prominent female flower (a stalked pistil); 1–2 or rarely 5 green kidney-shaped glands are positioned around the lip of the cup; true sepals and petals are absent, but leaves below the inflorescences are often pale green to nearly white at the base. Fruits are stalked, smooth to hairy, 3-lobed capsules containing 3 bumpy, white, brown, or dark-gray seeds.

Blooming Period
May–October.

Habitat
Dry, rocky, tallgrass prairies, pastures, roadsides, and disturbed sites; E ⅓.

Six-angled spurge (*E. hexagona* Nutt.) is an erect yellowish-green annual with linear to egg-shaped leaves and solitary inflorescences in the bases of upper leaves. It is found throughout most of the western two-thirds and infrequently in the eastern portion of our region, especially in sandy soil. Missouri spurge (*E. missurica* Raf.) is a smooth, spreading to erect, wiry-stemmed annual with linear leaves and solitary inflorescences at the bases of upper leaves, each with 4 prominent white or pinkish petal-like appendages with glands. It occurs throughout the region.

Croton texensis (Klotzsch) Muell. Arg.

Texas croton

Euphorbiaceae
Spurge Family

Description
Texas croton is a silvery, erect, annual herb ¾–2½ ft. tall and covered with a dense layer of star-shaped hairs. Stems are usually single and branched above.

Leaves are alternate, stalked, narrowly lance-shaped to elliptic, 1–3 in. long, and ¼–¾ in. wide, with entire margins. Inflorescences are compact racemes, and male and female flowers occur on separate plants. Male flowers have 5 sepals, no petals, and 8–12 stamens; female flowers have 5 sepals and no petals. Fruits are rounded, hairy, 3-lobed capsules containing 3 seeds.

Blooming Period
May–October.

Habitat
A wide range of prairie types, along roadsides, and on floodplains, especially in sandy soil; W ⅔.

One-seeded croton (*C. monanthogynus* Michx.) is a low annual found throughout the eastern two-thirds of the region. It grows on rocky to sandy prairies and in open woods, pastures, roadsides, and waste areas. It has tiny male and female flowers on the same plant and a single seed per capsule.

Croton capitatus Michx.

Woolly croton

Euphorbiaceae
Spurge Family

Description

Woolly croton is a silvery-green, erect, annual herb ½–3 ft. tall and covered with a dense woolly layer of star-shaped hairs. Stems are usually single but spreading-branched, especially in the upper half of the plant. Leaves are alternate, stalked, narrowly egg-shaped to elliptic, 1–4 in. long, and ¼–¾ in. wide, with entire margins. Inflorescences are short compact clusters near the ends of branches. The tiny male and female flowers are borne on the same plant; male flowers typically have 5 sepals and petals and 10–14 stamens; female flowers have 6–9 sepals and no petals. Fruits are rounded woolly capsules typically containing 3 seeds.

Blooming Period

June–October.

Habitat

A variety of prairies, open woods, pastures, roadsides, and waste areas, especially in rocky limestone soil; E ⅔ and rare in W.

Seeds of crotons are eaten by birds; however, seeds of some species contain poisonous oils.

Achillea millefolium L.

Yarrow

Asteraceae
Sunflower Family

Blooming Period
May–October.

Habitat
All prairie types, open woods, and open, somewhat disturbed areas; widespread but less frequent in W.

The flower heads can be air-dried for use in winter arrangements. This species has had many medicinal uses.

Description
Yarrow is an erect, woolly, somewhat aromatic, perennial herb ½–3 ft. tall. Stems are few-branched from a spreading rhizome. Leaves* are alternate, stalked to sessile, gradually reduced upward, 1–6 in. long, ¼–1 in. wide, and highly dissected, with a fernlike appearance. Inflorescences are flat-topped or domed clusters of tiny heads borne at the ends of stems. Disk and ray florets are white or infrequently pinkish; disk florets are usually 5 and about ⅛ in. long. Fruits are small, smooth, flattened achenes.

Erigeron bellidiastrum Nutt.

Western fleabane

Asteraceae
Sunflower Family

Description
Western fleabane is a finely hairy annual ¼–1½ ft. tall, arising from a slender taproot. Stems are spreading from the base and often multi-branched. Leaves are alternate, simple, stalked to sessile, and up to 2 in. long and ½ in. wide, with entire to toothed or slightly lobed margins; lower leaves are frequently absent on flowering plants. Inflorescences are numerous heads borne near the ends of branches. Bracts on heads are lance-shaped; ray florets are white to pink, numerous, linear, and less than ¼ in. long; disk florets are yellow. Fruits are short-hairy 2-ribbed achenes tipped with slender delicate bristles.

Blooming Period
June–August.

Habitat
Sandsage prairie and dry, sandy, short-grass and mixed prairies; W ½.

Erigeron and other members of the Asteraceae once were believed to repel fleas.

Western fleabane forms extensive populations on dunes along the Arkansas, Cimarron, and Canadian rivers. Fewer than 12 species of *Erigeron* occur in the region. Daisy fleabane (*E. strigosus* Muhl. ex Willd.) is an erect appressed-hairy annual with few leaves and is found on prairies in the eastern two-thirds of the region. A similar species in the eastern third is annual fleabane [*E. annuus* (L.) Pers.]. It has more numerous leaves and long spreading hairs.

Desmanthus illinoensis (Michx.) MacM.

Illinois bundleflower

Mimosaceae
Mimosa Family

Description
Illinois bundleflower is an erect, smooth to sparingly hairy, perennial herb 1–6 ft. tall, with a woody rootstock. Stems are somewhat woody, ridged, and angled. Leaves are alternate, stalked, 2–4 in. long, even-bipinnately compound with 6–16 segments, each with 15–30 pairs of small elliptic leaflets. Inflorescences are small, dense, spherical, headlike clusters on stalks arising from the bases of leaves. Flowers are small and 5-parted; the petals are whitish to tan; the 5 stamens have long filaments that give the inflorescences a fluffy appearance. Fruits* are flat, brown, crescent-shaped legumes that persist on the flowering stalks in dense clusters and contain 2–5 seeds.

Blooming Period
June–August.

Habitat
Rocky prairies, open wooded slopes, streambeds, roadsides, and disturbed sites; throughout region.

Illinois bundleflower is a highly palatable and nutritious legume that is consumed readily by livestock.

Two other bundleflowers occur in the region. Narrowpod bundleflower (*D. leptolobus* T. & G.) has 5 stamens per flower and straight fruits; it is scattered throughout the central two-thirds of the region. Cooley bundleflower [*D. cooleyi* (Eat.) Trel.] also has straight fruits, but there are 10 stamens in each flower; it occurs in the southwestern quarter of the region.

Asclepias arenaria Torr.

Sand milkweed

Asclepiadaceae
Milkweed Family

Blooming Period
June–August.

Habitat
Mixed, shortgrass, and sandsage prairies, usually in sandy soil; scattered over W ⅔.

Sand milkweed is especially common on sandy prairies associated with the major rivers of the region—for example, Arkansas, Cimarron, Canadian, and Red.

Dried pods (after seeds have dispersed) of all milkweeds are useful in arrangements and wreaths. Milkweeds are so named because of the milky sap that exudes from broken stems.

Description
Sand milkweed is a low perennial herb ½–2 ft. tall. Stems are hairy, branched, often reddish purple at the base and contain milky sap. Leaves are opposite, simple, fleshy, 1–5 in. long, ½–3 in. wide, and rectangular to egg-shaped, with short stalks. Inflorescences are umbels 1½–2½ in. across, arising from the bases of leaves, mostly on the upper half of the plant. Each umbel bears 25–50 hairy pinkish green to greenish white flowers, which are 5-parted with creamy white hoods and horns. Fruits* are broad, often hairy pods containing abundant seeds, each with a tuft of white or tan hairs at the tip.

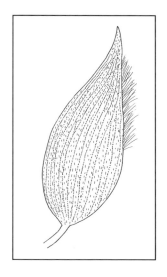

Asclepias viridiflora Raf.

Green milkweed

Asclepiadaceae
Milkweed Family

Description
Green milkweed is an erect perennial herb ½–3 ft. tall. Stems are sparingly to densely hairy and mostly unbranched and contain milky sap. Leaves* are mostly opposite, simple, leathery, linear to oval, 1½–5½ in. long, and ¼–2½ in. wide, often with wavy margins. Inflorescences are 1 to several dense umbels 1½–2½ in. across, arising from the bases of upper leaves. Each umbel bears 20–80 small, hairy, greenish white flowers, which are 5-parted with pale green sepals, greenish white to yellow petals, and similarly colored hoods lacking horns. Fruits are hairy pods containing numerous seeds, each with a tuft of tan hairs at the tip.

Blooming Period
June–August.

Habitat
All prairie types in sandy, clayey, and rocky limestone soils; throughout region.

Green milkweed exhibits remarkable variation in leaf shape, a trait that frequently causes consternation among beginning botanists and wildflower enthusiasts. However, the dense inflorescences and wavy leaf margins are rather reliable characters for identification.

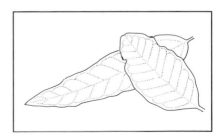

Asclepias engelmanniana Wood.

Engelmann's milkweed

Asclepiadaceae
Milkweed Family

Description

Engelmann's milkweed is a tall, slender, perennial herb 1–5 ft. tall. Stems are smooth or sparingly hairy and mostly branched and contain milky sap. Leaves are mostly alternate, simple, linear, droopy, 2–8 in. long, and less than ¼ in. wide. Inflorescences are umbels ½–1½ in. across, arising from the bases of leaves on the upper half of the plant. Each umbel contains 10–35 small, hairy, greenish white to yellowish white flowers, which are 5-parted with short white hoods and no horns. Fruits are slender, often hairy pods that contain numerous seeds, each with a tuft of white or tan hairs at the tip.

Blooming Period

June–August.

Habitat

Sandy or rocky limestone mixed and shortgrass prairies; W ⅔.

Engelmann's milkweed was named in honor of George Engelmann, an eminent nineteenth-century North American botanist. Narrow-leaved milkweed (*A. stenophylla* A. Gray), which may be mistaken for Engelmann's milkweed, occurs throughout all but the southwestern quarter of the region. It can be distinguished by the presence of horns in the flowers.

Asclepias verticillata L.

Whorled milkweed

Asclepiadaceae
Milkweed Family

and white hoods containing horns. Fruits are slender, slightly hairy pods containing numerous seeds, each with a tuft of white or tan hairs at the tip.

Blooming Period
June–September.

Habitat
Tallgrass, mixed, and infrequently shortgrass prairies in sandy, clayey, and rocky limestone soils; E ¾ but infrequent in W.

Poison milkweed [*A. subverticillata* (A. Gray) Vail] is highly toxic to livestock and frequently forms large patches along disturbed roadsides in the western quarter of the region. It differs from whorled milkweed in having short leafy shoots arising from the bases of leaves.

Description
Whorled milkweed is a slender, erect, perennial herb 1–3 ft. tall. Stems are sparingly hairy and mostly unbranched and contain milky sap. Leaves* are mostly in whorls, 3–6 per node, simple, linear, spreading, ½–3 in. long, and less than ¼ in. wide. Inflorescences are umbels ½–1½ in. across, arising from the bases of upper leaves. Each umbel contains 6–20 small, hairy, white to greenish white flowers, which are 5-parted with green sepals, white petals,

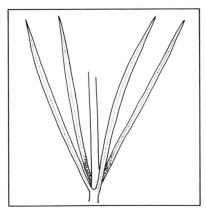

Saponaria officinalis L.

Soapwort,
Bouncing bet

Caryophyllaceae
Pink Family

Description

Soapwort is an erect, smooth, perennial herb 1–3 ft. tall. Stems are unbranched, with slightly swollen nodes, and often colonial from creeping rhizomes. Leaves are opposite, simple, stalked below to sessile above, with 3–5 veins, entire, thickish, lance-shaped to elliptic, 2–4 in. long, and ½–1 in. wide. Inflorescences are dense, few- to many-flowered, terminal clusters on short stalks arising from the bases of upper leaves. Flowers are showy, fragrant, and 5-parted; the calyx is green, tubular, and about 1 in. long; the 5 petals are white or pink; the 10 stamens project beyond the spreading petals. Fruits* are thin elongate capsules containing abundant small black seeds.

Blooming Period

June–September.

Habitat

Disturbed sites, roadsides, and waste places; NE ½ and infrequent in SW.

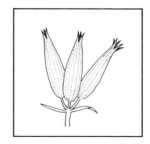

Sagittaria latifolia Willd.

Common arrowhead

Alismataceae
Water Plantain Family

¾ in. long; stamens are 25–40 with yellow anthers. Fruits* are flattened beaked achenes about ⅛ in. long and borne in heads up to 1 in. wide.

Blooming Period
June–September.

Habitat
Still or slowly flowing shallow water in ponds, streams, rivers, marshes, and ditches and on muddy shores; throughout region except SW ¼.

Description
Common arrowhead is an erect, smooth, aquatic, perennial herb with rhizomes and white fibrous roots. Leaves are basal, erect, long-stalked, and highly variable in shape, often arrowhead-shaped but occasionally lance-shaped, 2–30 in. long and 1–10 in. wide. Inflorescences are 1 to several, erect, racemelike, and on stalks ¼–4 ft. long and normally taller than the leaves. Flowers are in whorls of 2–15; lower whorls are of female flowers and upper whorls of male or perfect flowers; sepals are 3 and reflexed in fruit; the 3 white petals are showy and up to

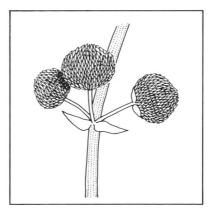

Hibiscus trionum L.

Flower-of-an-hour

Malvaceae
Mallow Family

Blooming Period
June–September.

Habitat
Disturbed sites, including pastures,
fields, roadsides, and waste areas; E ⅔
but less common in W.

This beautiful but sometimes bother-
some weed was introduced from Europe.
The common name refers to the usually
short time each flower remains open.
    Rose-of-Sharon (H. syriacus L.) is a
popular ornamental shrub native to eastern Asia. Okra (H. esculentus L.) is also
an Old World species. It is popular in
the southeastern United States, where the
fruits are consumed as vegetables.

Description
Flower-of-an-hour is an erect annual
herb ¼–2 ft. tall, with scattered simple
and star-shaped hairs.* Stems are single
and usually spreading-branched. Leaves
are alternate, stalked, ½–3 in. long, 1–
2½ in. wide, and palmately lobed, with
3–5 egg-shaped or wedge-shaped and
toothed segments. Flowers are solitary or
in small terminal clusters on short stalks
arising from the bases of leaves; the calyx
is 5-lobed, bristly, and membranelike,
with prominent veins; the corolla is
showy, 5-parted, and 1–2½ in. wide; the
petals are yellowish white with a reddish
purple base; the numerous reddish stamens are united into a column. Fruits*
are hairy, egg-shaped, 5-segmented capsules enclosed by the bladdery calyx;
each segment contains several dark
rough seeds.

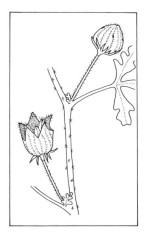

Cynanchum laeve (Michx.) Pers.

Sand vine,
Climbing milkweed

Asclepiadaceae
Milkweed Family

Description

Sand vine is a climbing or scrambling perennial vine, with milky sap. Stems are simple or branched, slender, somewhat hairy, and up to 20 ft. long. Leaves are opposite, simple, stalked, triangular to broadly egg-shaped or heart-shaped, 1–4 in. long, and ½–4 in. wide, with entire margins. Inflorescences are few-flowered panicles or umbel-like clusters arising on short stalks from the bases of leaves. Flowers are 5-parted, with whitish to greenish white lance-shaped petals; there are 5 stamens. Fruits* are long, smooth, tapered pods 3–5 in. long that contain many brownish flat seeds,* each with a tuft of white hairs at the tip.

Blooming Period

June–September.

Habitat

Forest margins, thickets, floodplains, and disturbed sites; E ½.

Convolvulus arvensis L.

Field bindweed

Convolvulaceae
Morning Glory Family

Blooming Period
June–September.

Habitat
Disturbed sites, including fields, pastures, roadsides, gardens, and waste areas; throughout region.

Description
Field bindweed is a twining or trailing perennial herb that often forms dense mats from creeping rhizomes. Stems are slender, branched, hairy, and up to 5 ft. long. Leaves are alternate, simple, arrowhead-shaped or sometimes heart-shaped, stalked, 1–3 in. long, and ½–2¼ in. wide. Flowers are 1 to several on long stalks arising from the bases of leaves; the calyx is 5-lobed; the corolla is funnel-shaped, slightly 5-angled, pleated, and white or pinkish, often with prominent pink bands. Fruits are small rounded capsules containing several dark seeds.

Field bindweed is an aggressive, troublesome weed that is difficult to eradicate because of its extensive system of rhizomes. It was introduced from Europe and is legally noxious in some states.

Gray bindweed (*C. equitans* Benth.) is a native species with grayish-hairy narrow leaves and a taproot. It occurs throughout the southwestern half of the region.

Hedge bindweed [*Calystegia sepium* (L.) R. Br.] was formerly included in this genus. It and related species are distinguished by larger flowers and the presence of leafy bracts at the base of the calyx.

Ipomoea pandurata (L.) G. F. Mey.

Bigroot morning-glory

Convolvulaceae
Morning Glory Family

Description

Bigroot morning-glory is a twining or trailing, smooth to sparsely hairy, perennial herb. Stems are sometimes branched and up to 10 ft. long and arise from an enlarged root. Leaves* are alternate, simple, entire, long-stalked, heart-shaped to egg-shaped, sometimes indented near the center or 3-lobed, 1–4 in. long, and about as wide. Flowers are solitary or several on stalks up to 8 in. long arising from the bases of leaves. The calyx is 5-lobed and thickish; the showy corolla is white with a lavender to reddish throat, funnel-shaped, slightly angular, pleated, and 2–3 in. long; stamens are 5. Fruits are smooth rounded capsules containing 1–4 woolly, brown, angular seeds.

Blooming Period

June–September.

Habitat

Roadsides, fencerows, fields, disturbed sites, and tallgrass prairies; E ⅓.

Morning-glories are named for the tendency of their flowers to open in the morning.

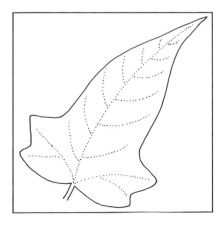

Euphorbia marginata Pursh

Snow-on-the-mountain

Euphorbiaceae
Spurge Family

Description
Snow-on-the-mountain is a stout, erect, smooth to spreading-hairy, annual herb 1–3½ ft. tall, with milky sap, arising from a taproot. Stems are single and branched. Leaves are alternate, simple, sessile, gradually reduced up the stem, lance-shaped to elliptic or egg-shaped, ¾–3½ in. long, ½–1½ in. wide, with entire margins. Inflorescences* are small cups borne in terminal clusters, each containing many tiny male flowers (single stamens) and a single prominent female flower (a stalked pistil); 3–5 greenish kidney-shaped glands associated with white petal-like appendages are positioned around the lip of the cup; true sepals and petals are absent, but leaves and bracts below the inflorescences bear broad white margins. Fruits are stalked, hairy, 3-lobed capsules containing 3 bumpy grayish seeds.

Blooming Period
June–October.

Habitat
All prairie types, pastures, roadsides, and waste areas, especially over limestone; throughout region.

Snow-on-the-mountain is available from seed catalogs to grow in the garden. Fire-on-the-mountain (*E. cyathophora* Murray) is an attractive annual with red or yellow patches near the bases of upper leaves and bracts. It occurs in the eastern third of the region and sporadically westward. Poinsettia (*E. pulcherrima* Willd.) is a popular Christmas ornamental cultivated for its bright red, pink, or white bracts. It is native to southern Mexico and Central America.

Euphorbia corollata L.

Flowering spurge

Euphorbiaceae
Spurge Family

Description

Flowering spurge is an erect, smooth to hairy, perennial herb ½–3½ ft. tall, with milky sap, arising from a stout root. Stems are 1 to several and mostly spreading-branched above. Leaves are alternate, simple, short-stalked or sessile, often crowded, gradually reduced up the stem, lance-shaped to elliptic, ½–3 in. long, and less than ¾ in. wide, with entire margins. Inflorescences are numerous small flowerlike cups borne at the ends of branches, each containing many tiny male flowers (single stamens) and a single prominent female flower (a stalked pistil); 5 yellowish green kidney-shaped glands associated with white petal-like appendages are positioned around the lip

of the cup, true sepals and petals are absent. Fruits are stalked, smooth, 3-lobed capsules containing 3 smooth whitish-gray seeds.

Blooming Period
June–October.

Habitat
Dry, rocky tallgrass prairies, pastures, roadsides, and disturbed sites; E ⅓.

The highly modified inflorescences of spurges are called cyathia. Mature fruits and seeds are often needed to identify many of the 27 species in the region. The sap of euphorbias can cause skin irritation.

Phytolacca americana L.

Pokeweed,
Pokeberry

Phytolaccaceae
Pokeweed Family

Description
Pokeweed is a smooth, often robust, annual herb that grows up to 10 ft. tall. Stems are 1 to several, branched above, red to purple, and up to 1½ in. in diameter. Leaves are alternate, simple, stalked, lance-shaped or broader, entire, 4–15 in. long, and 2–6 in. wide. Inflorescences are curved racemes up to 8 in. long arising from the bases of upper leaves. Flowers are about ¼ in. across, with 5 greenish white to pink sepals, no petals, and 10 stamens. Fruits are dark purple juicy berries over ¼ in. in diameter that contain small, shiny, black seeds.

Blooming Period
June–October.

Habitat
Disturbed sites in rich soil, including gardens, pastures, fields, thickets, low woods, roadsides, and waste areas; E ½.

Young leaves of pokeweed are used as a common potherb in the southern United States. The plant was immortalized in a song by Tony Joe White that recounted the misfortunes of Pokesalad Annie. Although poisonous to humans, the berries are eaten by many birds. Juice from the berries has been used as ink or dye. The term "poke" denotes a plant used in dyeing.

Mollugo verticillata L.

Carpetweed

Molluginaceae
Carpetweed Family

Description
Carpetweed is a low, spreading, smooth, annual herb that lies flat on the ground and has a slender taproot. Stems are multi-branched and slender. Leaves are in whorls of 3–8, simple, short-stalked to sessile, entire, lance-shaped to narrowly spatula-shaped, ½–1 in. long, and mostly less than ½ in. wide. Inflorescences are clusters of 2–6 flowers* on threadlike stalks up to ½ in. long, arising from the nodes. Sepals are 5, tiny, somewhat petal-like, and pale green to white; petals are absent; stamens are 3–4. Fruits are small egg-shaped capsules containing numerous tiny, kidney-shaped, brownish seeds.

Blooming Period
June–October.

Habitat
Disturbed sites, including fields, pastures, roadsides, stream and riverbanks, and waste areas, especially on open sandy ground; throughout region but infrequent in W ⅕.

The common name is a reference to the plant's habit of growing in dense carpet-like patches.

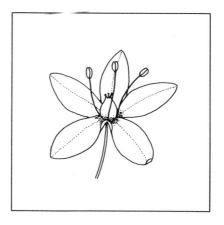

Heliotropium convolvulaceum (Nutt.) A. Gray

Bindweed heliotrope,
Wild heliotrope

Boraginaceae
Borage Family

Description

Bindweed heliotrope is a short, grayish, appressed-hairy annual, mostly less than 8 in. tall, with a slender taproot. Stems are prostrate or ascending and branched from the base. Leaves are alternate, simple, stalked, ½–1½ in. long, less than ½ in. wide, lance-shaped to egg-shaped, and entire. Inflorescences are short coiled clusters at the ends of branches. Sepals are 5-lobed and appressed-hairy; the white or bluish white corolla is funnel shaped and ¼–¾ in. wide; stamens are 5. Fruits are groups of 4 small smooth nutlets, each containing a single seed.

Blooming Period
June–October.

Habitat
Sand and sandsage prairies, especially on sandhills and along sandy riverbeds; SW ½.

Pasture heliotrope [*H. tenellum* (Nutt.) Torr.] is found on rocky limestone prairies and in woodlands in the southeastern quarter of the region. It has smaller solitary flowers arising from the bases of linear leaves. Seaside heliotrope (*H. curassavicum* L.) is a succulent smooth plant known from scattered sites in the central third of the region, where it inhabits damp saline soils in marshes and salt flats.

Asclepias latifolia (Torr.) Raf.

Broadleaf milkweed

Asclepiadaceae
Milkweed Family

Habitat
Sandy, clayey, and rocky limestone soils in mixed and shortgrass prairies; W ½.

Broadleaf milkweed is among the most common and widespread of the milkweeds in the southern High Plains. The species is a prominent herb on shortgrass prairies but is poisonous to livestock.

Description
Broadleaf milkweed is a stout, erect, perennial herb ½–2 ft. tall. Stems are generally short-hairy, unbranched, and reddish purple and contain copious milky sap. Leaves are opposite, simple, stalked, fleshy, somewhat waxy, egg-shaped to elliptic, 2–6 in. long, 1–5 in. wide, and hairy, especially beneath. Inflorescences are spherical umbels that are up to 3 in. across and arise from the bases of upper leaves. Each umbel contains 20–60 yellowish green flowers, which are 5-parted with yellowish white to yellowish green hoods and pale horns. Fruits* are large hairless pods up to 5 in. long that contain numerous seeds, each with a tuft of long tan hairs at the tip.

Blooming Period
July–August.

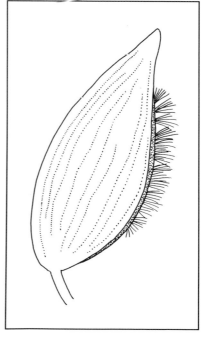

Cicuta maculata L.

Common water hemlock

Apiaceae
Parsley Family

Blooming Period
July–August.

Habitat
Wet sites, including marshes, moist prairies and pastures, stream and riverbanks, ponds, and ditches; scattered throughout most of region but most abundant in E ½.

This is a highly poisonous species. The branched fleshy roots and hollow stem help distinguish this plant from others with edible roots.

Description
Common water hemlock is a stout, erect, perennial herb 3–7 ft. tall, with fleshy fingerlike roots. Stems are smooth and often waxy, hollow, and sometimes purple-spotted. Leaves are alternate, stalked, 8–20 in. long, and 2–3 times pinnately compound with narrowly lance-shaped leaflets* bearing small scattered teeth. Inflorescences are flat or rounded, open, compound umbels 2–5 in. across; the smaller umbels have long and spreading stalks. The tiny white flowers are 5-parted. Fruits are rounded, with 2 small, dry, ribbed segments.

Mentzelia nuda (Pursh) T. & G.

Sand lily,
Bractless mentzelia

Loasaceae
Stickleaf Family

Description

Sand lily is an erect, coarse, rough-hairy, biennial or perennial herb 1–5 ft. tall, with a taproot. Stems are 1 to few, usually branched above, and whitish. Leaves are alternate, simple, short-stalked below to sessile above, 1½–4 in. long, and ½–1 in. wide, with coarsely toothed margins. Inflorescences are few-flowered clusters borne near the ends of branches. Flowers are 2–4 in. wide, opening in the afternoon and closing around sunset; the sepals are 5, lance-shaped, and up to 1 in. long; petals are mostly 10, white, up to 2 in. long, somewhat spatula-shaped, and generally not touching when the flower is open; stamens are abundant and mixed with many threadlike sterile stamens. Fruits* are cylindrical 1 in.-long capsules with dried sepals at the top and contain numerous winged seeds.

Blooming Period
July–September.

Habitat
Mixed, shortgrass, and sandsage prairies, pastures, and roadsides, especially in sandy soil; W ½.

Sand lily is not related to true lilies.

Ten-petal mentzelia [M. *decapetala* (Pursh) Urban & Gilg] is very similar to the sand lily and occurs throughout the same area. It has petals that are 1–3 in. long, cream-colored, and touching or overlapping when the flowers are open. Additionally, it tends to favor a more solid footing, especially on rocky slopes and outcrops.

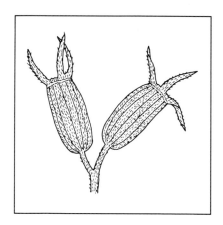

Lespedeza capitata Michx.

Round-head lespedeza,
Bush clover

Fabaceae
Bean Family

Description
Round-head lespedeza is an erect, appressed-hairy, perennial herb 1½–3 ft.
tall, arising from a woody, branched
rootstock. Stems are 1 to several, mostly
unbranched, and rigid. Leaves are alternate, short-stalked to sessile, often
crowded, with 3 elliptic to wedge-shaped
leaflets 1–2 in. long and less than ½ in.
wide. Inflorescences are crowded, round
to cylindrical, leafy, terminal racemes.
The calyx has 5 pointed lobes; petals are
white to yellowish white, the upper one
with a reddish purple spot at the base;
stamens are 10, with 9 joined by their filaments and 1 free. Fruits* are short leg-

umes surrounded by the persistent calyx
and containing a single brownish, shiny,
flattened seed.

Blooming Period
July–September.

Habitat
Tallgrass, mixed, and sand prairies, roadsides, and occasionally in open dry
woods; E ½.

Slender lespedeza [*L. virginica* (L.) Britt.]
is a native perennial with pink or violet
flowers. It occurs in prairies and open
woods in the southeastern quarter of the
region and will hybridize with round-
head lespedeza. Prairie lespedeza [*L. vio-
lacea* (L.) Pers.] is also a native perennial
but has slender branched stems, elliptic
to egg-shaped leaflets, and violet flowers.
It is found in prairies and open dry
woods in the eastern quarter of the region. Branches of lespedeza fruits can be
used in dried-flower arrangements.

Datura stramonium L.

Jimson weed

Solanaceae
Nightshade Family

Description
Jimson weed is a coarse, taprooted, annual herb that grows up to 4 ft. tall. Stems are erect, branched, and scarcely to densely hairy. Leaves are alternate, simple, stalked, broadly lance-shaped to egg-shaped, 3–12 in. long, 1–9 in. wide, usually dark green but very young leaves are frequently downy white, and with wavy or toothed margins. Flowers are solitary, generally erect, and arise from the bases of upper leaves; the calyx is 5-lobed and up to 2 in. long; the corolla is trumpetlike, 5-angled, 2½–4 in. long, and white or violet-tinged; there are 5 stamens. Fruits* are large, spiny, egg-shaped capsules containing abundant small black seeds.

Blooming Period
July–September.

Habitat
Disturbed habitats, particularly feedlots, heavily grazed pastures, waste ground, and floodplains; all but NW ¼.

Jimson weed was introduced from the American tropics and is well known for its poisonous and narcotic properties. "Jimson" is a corruption of "Jamestown" (Virginia), where this plant was first collected in the early 1800s.
  Sacred datura (*Datura innoxia* P. Mill) and oak-leaved datura (*D. quercifolia* H.B.K.) also occur in the region and are poisonous.

Cuscuta glomerata Choisy

Cluster dodder

Cuscutaceae
Dodder Family

Description

Cluster dodder is a twining parasitic herb without obvious leaves. Stems are slender and white to yellowish orange. Inflorescences are dense ropelike masses of tiny flowers wound around the stem of the host plant. The calyx is 5-parted, with separate sepals. The corolla is white, urnlike, and 4-lobed, with spreading or reflexed tips; there are 5 stamens. Fruits are small spherical capsules usually containing 4 brownish rounded seeds.

Blooming Period

July–September.

Habitat

Tallgrass and mixed prairies, open disturbed sites, and thickets, usually on members of the Sunflower Family; E ⅔.

Dodders take water and nutrients from their host plants by means of small peglike structures that penetrate the stem tissues. The root of the dodder dies once a parasitic relationship has been established. Some dodders exhibit a preference for specific hosts, but most parasitize a wide range of species. Other common names for dodders include love vine, angels' hair, strangle vine, and witches' shoelaces. Dodder can be used to make a yellow dye.

Lycopus americanus Muhl. ex Bart.

American bugleweed

Lamiaceae
Mint Family

pale pink, and sometimes with small purplish spots within; there are 2 stamens. Fruits are composed of 4 small smooth nutlets, each containing a single seed.

Blooming Period
July–October.

Habitat
Low, wet ground around ponds, lakes, marshes, ditches, streams, and rivers; throughout region.

Five species of bugleweed occur in the region. American bugleweed is the most common and widespread. Virginia bugleweed (*L. virginicus* L.), occasionally encountered in the northeastern quarter of the region, has nutlets that are bumpy and longer than the lobes of the calyx.

Description
American bugleweed is an ascending to erect, smooth to hairy, perennial herb ½–3 ft. tall, with branched, creeping rhizomes. Stems are 1 to several, sometimes branched, and 4-angled. Leaves are opposite, simple, short-stalked to sessile, gland-dotted, lance-shaped to elliptic, ½–3 in. long, and ¼–1 in. wide, with nearly entire to coarsely toothed margins. Inflorescences are small dense clusters of flowers* borne at the bases of leaves. The calyx is 5-lobed; the corolla is 4-lobed, funnel-shaped, white to very

Penthorum sedoides L.

Ditch stonecrop

Crassulaceae
Stonecrop Family

Description
Ditch stonecrop is an erect, smooth, shiny, perennial herb ½–2½ ft. tall, with slender rhizomes and fibrous roots. Stems are 1 to several and sometimes few-branched. Leaves are alternate, simple, stalked, often turning orange or reddish with age, lance-shaped to ellip-tic, 1–9 in. long, and ½–1½ in. wide with toothed margins. Inflorescences are glandular-hairy, 2–6 branched, elongate, slightly coiled clusters borne at the ends of branches; flowers are produced on the upper side of the branches. Sepals are 5 or rarely 6–7, light green to yellowish green, and erect or spreading; petals are absent; stamens are 10. Fruits* are angu-lar, 5-horned, 5-segmented capsules that contain many orangish seeds.

Blooming Period
July–October.

Habitat
Moist to wet ground along streams and rivers, around ponds, and in ditches and marshes; E ½ and infrequently in W.

Gaura longiflora Spach

Large-flowered gaura

Onagraceae
Evening Primrose Family

Description
Large-flowered gaura is a robust, erect, densely hairy and sometimes sticky, annual herb 1½–7 ft. tall. Stems are usually single, branched above, and arise from a fleshy taproot. Leaves are alternate, simple, sessile, lance-elliptic to elliptic, 1–5 in. long, and mostly less than 1 in. wide, with entire to shallowly toothed margins. Inflorescences are multi-branched, hairy, sticky spikes. Flowers have a slender floral tube atop the ovary; sepals are 4 and reflexed; petals are 4, white to pale pink, and up to ½ in. long; stamens are 8, with yellow or red anthers. Fruits are angular elongate capsules containing 2–4 brownish seeds.

Blooming Period
July–October.

Habitat
Rocky tallgrass prairies, roadsides, disturbed sites, and infrequently in wooded areas; E ½.

Aster ericoides L.

Heath aster,
White aster

Asteraceae
Sunflower Family

Description
Heath aster is a hairy, colonial, perennial herb 1–3 ft. tall. Stems are spreading to erect and few to many arising from a rhizome or woody rootstock. Leaves are alternate, simple, mostly linear, entire, ses- sile, ½–1½ in. long, and less than ¼ in. wide; lower leaves usually are absent on flowering plants. Inflorescences are panicles of few to many, small, cylindrical to bell-shaped heads borne mostly on one side of the branches. Ray florets are 10–20, white, and less than ½ in. long; disk florets are yellow. Fruits are small, brownish, appressed-hairy achenes tipped with abundant slender whitish bristles.

Blooming Period
August–October.

Habitat
All prairie types; throughout region.

Aster is a large, complicated genus with more than two dozen species represented in the region. White prairie aster [*A. falcatus* Lindl. subsp. *commutatus* (T. & G.) A. G. Jones] is a similar species found in the western half of the region on mixed and shortgrass prairies. It has larger heads that are evenly distributed around the ends of branches.

Eupatorium altissimum L.

Tall joe-pye weed

Asteraceae
Sunflower Family

Description
Tall joe-pye weed is an erect, smooth to soft spreading-hairy, perennial herb 2–6 ft. tall, with spreading rhizomes. Stems are 1 to several. Leaves are opposite, simple, short-stalked to sessile, prominently 3-nerved, glandular-dotted, narrowly elliptic to narrowly lance-shaped, 2–5 in. long, and ¼–1 in. wide, with toothed margins, especially toward the tip. Inflorescences are panicle-like clusters of many small cylindrical heads. Bracts of the heads are lance-shaped; ray florets are absent; disk florets are 5, white, and glandular-dotted. Fruits are small, angular, brown or black achenes with slender bristles at the tip.

Blooming Period
August–October.

Habitat
Tallgrass prairies, pastures, roadsides, and disturbed sites, often in rocky limestone soil; E ⅓.

Joe Pye was an Indian (possibly fictional) in New England who cured typhus with another species of *Eupatorium*.

Tall joe-pye weed is occasionally confused with false boneset (*Kuhnia eupatorioides* L.); however, the latter has alternate leaves and 10-ribbed achenes. White snakeroot (*E. rugosum* Houtt.) occurs in open woods and disturbed sites in the eastern third of the region; it has 12–24 white florets per head and broadly egg-shaped leaves. Boneset (*E. perfoliatum* L.) has drooping opposite leaves joined at the bases and is found over the eastern half of the region,

Kuhnia eupatorioides L.

False boneset

Asteraceae
Sunflower Family

stout woody root. Leaves are numerous, alternate, simple, short-stalked, lance-shaped, 1–4 in. long, ¼–1½ in. wide with entire or toothed margins and covered with small glandular dots on the lower surface. Inflorescences are open, panicle-like clusters of cylindrical heads borne at the ends of branches. Bracts on the heads are lance-shaped and stiff; ray florets are absent; disk florets are whitish to yellowish white. Fruits are small ribbed achenes tipped with feathery bristles.

Blooming Period
August–October.

Habitat
All prairie types, especially in sandy or rocky soil; throughout region.

Description
False boneset is a nearly smooth to densely short-hairy perennial herb 1–3 ft. tall. Stems are one to several from a

Kuhnia is occasionally included in the genus *Brickellia* by some authors. This plant resembles boneset, a species of *Eupatorium* with many medicinal uses.

Spiranthes cernua (L.) Rich.

Lady's tresses

Orchidaceae
Orchid Family

Description
Lady's tresses is an erect perennial herb ¼–2 ft. tall, with slender fleshy roots. Stems are single, unbranched, and smooth to short-hairy. Leaves are mostly basal, alternate, simple, sessile, entire, fleshy, linear to lance-shaped, 2–12 in. long, and ½–1 in. wide. Inflorescences are stout terminal spikes with few to many ¼ in.–long flowers* arranged in 2–3 tight spirals. Sepals are 3, white, and petal-like; the 3 petals are white or creamy, the lower one liplike, thick, slightly constricted near the middle, and with a yellowish green center; the single stamen is highly modified and joined to the pistil. Fruits* are erect egg-shaped capsules containing abundant minute seeds.

Blooming Period
August–November.

Habitat
Tallgrass, mixed, and sand prairies; E ½.

The common name refers to the shape of the inflorescence, which resembles a woman's braided hair.

Great Plains lady's tresses (*S. magnicamporum* Sheviak) is easily confused with this species, but its leaves are usually absent at flowering, the lip lacks a constriction at the middle, and it tends to inhabit drier sites. Slender lady's tresses [*S. lacera* (Raf.) Raf.] is a graceful plant with a single spiral of delicate ¼ in.–long flowers bearing wavy greenish white lips.

Pink, Red, or Brown

Claytonia virginica L.

Virginia spring beauty

Portulacaceae
Purslane Family

Description
Virginia spring beauty is a succulent, smooth, perennial herb 4–12 in. tall, with a rounded corm. Leaves are mostly basal, simple, stalked, linear to lance-shaped, 2½–8 in. long, and ¼–½ in. wide, with entire margins; stem leaves are opposite and smaller. Inflorescences are racemes of 5–20 flowers. The calyx consists of 2 sepals; the 5 oval petals are about ½ in. long and white to pink, with reddish or purple veins; there are 5 stamens. Fruits are small rounded capsules containing small, dark, shiny seeds.

Blooming Period
February–July.

Habitat
Upland and bottomland forests, thickets, clearings, fields, and infrequently tallgrass prairies in short vegetation; E ¼.

The genus *Claytonia* was described by Carl Linnaeus in honor of John Clayton, an eighteenth-century North American botanist who studied the plants of Virginia.

Lamium amplexicaule L.

Henbit

Lamiaceae
Mint Family

long, and soft-hairy; the 4 stamens have orangish anthers. Fruits are composed of 4 small spotted nutlets, each containing a single seed.

Blooming Period
March–May, occasionally also in late fall, especially in warm protected sites.

Habitat
Disturbed sites, including fields, lawns, roadsides, pastures, and waste areas; E ⅓.

This common but attractive weed was introduced from Europe and is naturalized throughout much of North America. It often forms dense purple stands in fields in the spring.

Dead nettle or purple dead nettle (*L. purpureum* L.) is also a weedy annual naturalized in the eastern quarter of the region. It has egg-shaped to triangular bracts that are stalked.

Description
Henbit is a low, smooth to short-hairy, winter annual ¼–1 ft. tall, with a slender taproot. Stems are creeping to erect, few to many, and branched from the base. Leaves* are opposite, simple, long-stalked below but sessile and clasping above, crowded toward the ends of branches, rounded to broadly egg-shaped, and ¼–¾ in. long, with blunt-toothed or lobed margins. Inflorescences are congested, distinct, leafy-bracted clusters of flowers borne at the ends of branches. The calyx is 5-lobed and densely hairy; the corolla is 2-lipped, pale pink to pinkish purple, lobes and throat often purple spotted, ½–¾ in.

allirhoe alcaeoides (Michx.) A. Gray

Pink poppy mallow

Malvaceae
Mallow Family

Description

Pink poppy mallow is a spreading peren-nial herb ½–2 ft. tall, with a thick turnip-like rootstock. Stems are few to many, branched from the base, and hairy. Leaves are alternate, simple, stalked, 1½–4 in. long, 1–3 in. wide, and pal-mately lobed; basal leaves are often less deeply lobed. Flowers are solitary or in small groups on stalks up to 4 in. long; the calyx is 5-lobed; the 5 petals are ½–1 in long and pale pink or white; the nu-merous stamens are united in a column.* Fruits are rings of 10–15 beaked kidney-shaped segments, each containing a single seed.

Blooming Period

March–August.

Habitat

Dry, rocky, or sandy soils on tallgrass and mixed prairies; E ½.

Callirhoe is a small genus of about a dozen species restricted to temperate North America and most diverse in the central United States.

Callirhoe involucrata (T. & G.) A. Gray

Purple poppy mallow

Malvaceae
Mallow Family

Description
Purple poppy mallow is an attractive, spreading, perennial herb, with a woody root. Stems are several to many, branched, usually hairy, and up to 3 ft. long. Leaves are alternate, simple, stalked, 1½–3½ in. long, 1–3 in. wide, and deeply, palmately lobed, with linear segments. Flowers are solitary on stalks up to 8 in. long and often numerous; the calyx is 5-lobed, with 3 small leafy bracts; the 5 petals are rose to purple and 1–2½ in. long; the numerous stamens are united into a column. Fruits* are rings of 15–25 prominently beaked kidney-shaped segments, each containing a single seed.

Blooming Period
March–October.

Habitat
Dry open prairies of all types, especially in sandy soil, pastures, roadsides, and open woods; throughout region.

This species is a frequent inhabitant of roadsides in the western part of the region, where mowing may stimulate the production of numerous stems and masses of flowers. The color turns to blue-purple when the flowers are pressed, but the satiny texture remains.

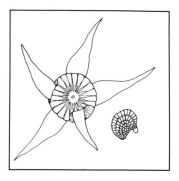

Verbena canadensis (L.) Britt.

Rose verbena

Verbenaceae
Vervain Family

Description

Rose verbena is a low, spreading or ascending, somewhat hairy, perennial herb. Stems are several to many, multibranched from the base, 1–2 ft. long, and often rooting at the nodes. Leaves* are opposite, stalked, egg-shaped to lance-shaped in outline, ½–4 in. long, and ½–2 in. wide, with toothed to pinnately 3-lobed margins. Inflorescences are showy terminal spikes that are flattened at first but elongate in fruit. Flowers are 5-lobed; the calyx is over ¼ in. long and glandular-hairy, with uneven slender lobes; the corolla is pink to rose, sometimes tinged purple, tubular, and about ½ in. wide, with spreading lobes; the 4 stamens are in 2 groups of different lengths. Fruits are composed of 4 slender, gray to black, ridged nutlets, each containing a single seed.

Blooming Period

March–October.

Habitat

Tallgrass prairies, pastures, roadsides, and open woods, especially in rocky soil; E ⅓.

Allium perdulce S. V. Fraser

Plains wild onion

Liliaceae
Lily Family

Description
Plains wild onion is an erect perennial herb ¼–¾ ft. tall, with leaves and flowering stalk arising from a bulb. The plant has an onionlike odor, especially when crushed. Leaves are 3 or more, linear, channeled, and as long as or longer than the flowering stalk. Inflorescences are erect umbels of 3–20 small, urn-shaped, pink to deep rose flowers; the 3 sepals and 3 petals are similar in color and texture. Fruits are small rounded capsules containing few black seeds and surrounded by the persistent petals and sepals.

Blooming Period
April–June.

Habitat
Mixed, shortgrass, and sand prairies; C ⅓.

Ten species of *Allium* occur in the region. Wild onion, or Canada onion (*A. canadense* L.), is the most widespread and variable. It is taller than the plains wild onion, has petals and sepals that wither away from the fruit, and sometimes produces small bulblets in place of flowers. Drummond's wild onion (*A. drummondii* Regel) is widespread in the central two-thirds of the region and has petals and sepals that become rigid and spread outward when the plant is in fruit.

Oxalis violacea L.

Violet wood sorrel

Oxalidaceae
Wood Sorrel Family

Description

Violet wood sorrel is a low, stemless, smooth, colonial, perennial herb, with a scaly bulb. Leaves are basal and long-stalked, 2–5 in. long, with 3 triangular to heart-shaped, ¼–¾ in.–long, ½–1 in.–wide, gray-green, somewhat waxy leaflets. Inflorescences are terminal umbels of 4–15 flowers on naked stalks 2–7 in. long. Sepals are 5, with orange tips; petals are 5, purplish pink to lavender, and ¼–½ in. long; stamens are 10, with 5 long ones alternating with 5 shorter ones. Fruits are ¼ in.–long egg-shaped capsules containing numerous small orangish seeds.

Blooming Period

April–June; often reflowering in September–October.

Habitat

Tallgrass and mixed prairies, roadsides, and open woods, often in rocky soil; E ½.

The term "sorrel" is used for several plants with a sour juice. Leaves of sorrels fold up at night and on cloudy days.

Three other sorrels, all yellow-flowered, occur in the region. Yellow wood sorrel (*O. stricta* L.) and gray-green wood sorrel (*O. dillenii* Jacq.) both occur in the eastern half of the region and have ascending stems. Creeping ladies sorrel (*O. corniculata* L.) is a common greenhouse weed with creeping stems rooting at the nodes.

Penstemon cobaea Nutt.

Cobaea beardtongue,
Cobaea penstemon

Scrophulariaceae
Figwort Family

Description

Cobaea beardtongue is a robust, erect, perennial herb ½–3½ ft. tall, with a stout woody rootstock. Stems are 1 to several, unbranched, and short-hairy below and glandular-hairy above, especially in the inflorescence. Leaves are opposite, simple, stalked below but sessile and clasping above, obscurely to sharply toothed, smooth to short-hairy, spatula-shaped below to lance-shaped or egg-shaped above, 1½–10 in. long, and ½–3 in. wide. Inflorescences are narrow panicles up to 20 in. long, with large showy flowers. The calyx is 5-lobed and sticky-glandular; the corolla is inflated, up to 2½ in. long, and 2-lipped, with 2 upper lobes and 3 lower lobes, sticky-glandular, and pale pink to white with violet lines within; the 5 stamens* include a sterile one bearded with yellow hairs at the tip. Fruits are woody egg-shaped capsules containing numerous small, angular, black seeds.

Blooming Period
April–June.

Habitat
Tallgrass and mixed prairies, roadsides, and pastures, especially in rocky limestone and gypsum soils; E ½.

This attractive species is particularly common in the Flint Hills region. Cobaea beardtongue was named for the resemblance of its flowers to those of the cup and saucer plant (*Cobaea scandens* Cav.), a climbing ornamental in the Phlox Family.

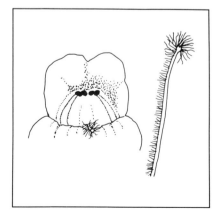

illardia pulchella Fouq.

Rose-ring gaillardia,
Indian blanket flower

Asteraceae
Sunflower Family

Description

Rose-ring gaillardia is an erect, rough-hairy, somewhat glandular, annual herb ¼–2 ft. tall, arising from a taproot. Stems are single and typically multi-branched. Leaves are alternate, simple, sessile and often clasping, lance-shaped to egg-shaped, 1–4 in. long, and ¼–1 in. wide, with entire, toothed, or lobed margins. Inflorescences are mostly solitary heads, 1–2 in. wide, on long stalks. Bracts on the heads are lance-shaped; ray florets are ½–1 in. long and up to ¼ in. wide, yellow at the tip and red to reddish purple toward the base or rarely yellow throughout, and prominently 3-lobed at the tip; disk florets are brownish purple and intermixed with numerous long stiff bristles. Fruits are short dark achenes bearing a tuft of hairs at the base and a crown of long pointed scales at the tip.

Blooming Period

April–September.

Habitat

Mixed, shortgrass, and sandsage prairies, especially in sandy soil; W ⅘ but more common in W.

This attractive wildflower often forms dense, colorful stands that may be visible from some distance.

Prairie gaillardia [*G. aestivalis* (Walt.) Rock] occurs in the central third of the region and has small soft bristles scattered among the disk florets. Rayless gaillardia [*G. suavis* (A. Gray & Engelm.) Britt. & Rusby] has ray florets that are absent or inconspicuous. It is found mostly in the southern half of the region.

Gaura coccinea Pursh

Scarlet gaura

Onagraceae
Evening Primrose Family

Flowers have a slender floral tube atop the ovary; sepals are 4 and reflexed; petals are 4, pink, reddish orange, or white, and less than ¼ in. long; stamens are 8, with red anthers. Fruits* are short spindle-shaped capsules containing 1–4 reddish-brown seeds.

Blooming Period
April–September.

Habitat
Dry rocky to sandy prairies, stream valleys, and roadsides; W ⅔.

Description
Scarlet gaura is a low, hairy, often colonial, perennial herb ¾–1½ ft. tall, arising from a woody spreading rootstalk. Stems usually are several and branched above. Leaves are alternate, simple, linear to narrowly elliptic, ¼–2 in. long, and mostly less than ½ in. wide, with entire to shallowly toothed margins. Inflorescences are terminal spikes 2–20 in. long.

Schrankia nuttallii (DC.) Standl.

Catclaw sensitive brier

Mimosaceae
Mimosa Family

are slender, ribbed, dry, prickly legumes 1–5 in. long that contain many ⅛ in.–long seeds.

Blooming Period
April–September.

Habitat
Nearly all prairie types, roadsides, and open woods, especially in sandy or rocky soil; throughout region but infrequent in W ⅕.

Western sensitive brier [*S. occidentalis* (Woot. & Standl.) Standl.] has seeds about ¼ in. long and young stems, stalks, and leaves that are usually short-hairy. It inhabits sandy or rocky short-grass prairies in the southwestern quarter of the region. Both species have leaflets that respond to touch by folding inward.

Description
Catclaw sensitive brier is a sprawling or arched perennial herb that bears many short recurved prickles. Stems are 1–7 ft. long, ribbed, and arise from a woody rootstalk. Leaves are alternate, stalked, 2–4½ in. long, and even bipinnately compound with 3–8 segments, each with 12–16 pairs of small elliptic leaflets. Inflorescences are showy, dense, spherical, headlike clusters on stalks ¾–1½ in. long arising from the bases of leaves. Flowers are small, pink, and 5-parted; the 8–12 stamens have long pink filaments and yellow anthers that give the inflorescence a fluffy appearance. Fruits*

Malva neglecta Wallr.

Common mallow

Malvaceae
Mallow Family

Description
Common mallow is a creeping to erect, annual or perennial herb ½–3 ft. tall, often densely covered with star-shaped hairs and some simple hairs. Stems are slender, usually branched, and arise from a deep root. Leaves are alternate, simple, stalked, rounded to kidney-shaped, 1–4 in. long, ½–3 in. wide, and typically with 5–9 shallow lobes and toothed margins. Flowers are in groups of 1–3 on stalks up to 2 in. long arising from the bases of leaves. The calyx is 5-lobed; the corolla is 5-parted, white to pink, occasionally with darker veins, and ½–¾ in. wide; the numerous pink stamens are united into a column. Fruits* are rings of 10–20 smooth, kidney-shaped segments containing brownish seeds.

Blooming Period
April–October.

Habitat
Disturbed sites, including pastures, fields, lawns, roadsides, and waste areas; widely scattered throughout region but less common in W.

Common mallow is an Old World species once used as a food and medicinal plant. It is naturalized throughout much of North America.

Round-leaf mallow (M. *rotundifolia* L.) is very similar, with slightly smaller flowers and pitted fruit segments. It is found in the northeastern half of the region and was also introduced from Europe.

Talinum calycinum Engelm.

Rockpink fameflower

Portulacaceae
Purslane Family

Description
Rockpink fameflower is a succulent, smooth, perennial herb 2–10 in. tall, with a thick brownish rootstock. Leaves are alternate, simple, fleshy, narrowly cylindrical, 1–3 in. long, and less than ⅛ in. wide. Inflorescences are few-flowered terminal clusters on slender stalks up to 10 in. long. Flowers have 2 sepals; the 8–10 petals are bright pink or red, broadly elliptic, and about ½ in. long; the stamens are numerous. Fruits* are small spherical capsules containing tiny, smooth, black seeds.

Blooming Period
May–June.

Habitat
Tallgrass, mixed, shortgrass, and sand prairies, especially in sandy or gravelly soil; scattered throughout most of region but less common in W.

Populations of rockpink fameflower tend to be closely associated with sandstone outcrops or wind-blown sand deposits.
  Prairie fameflower (*T. parviflorum* Nutt.) occurs in sandy soil in the southeastern quarter of the region. It has petals usually less than ¼ in. long and fewer stamens than the rockpink fameflower.

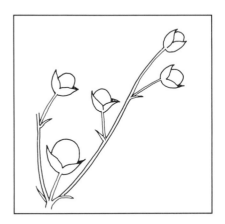

Phlox pilosa L.

Prairie phlox

Polemoniaceae
Phlox Family

Description
Prairie phlox is an erect, hairy or glandular-hairy, perennial herb ½–2½ ft. tall, with a stout rootstock. Stems are 1 to several and sometimes branched. Leaves are opposite, simple, sessile, entire, linear to lance-shaped or narrowly egg-shaped, 1–4 in. long, and ¼–1 in. wide. Inflorescences are terminal compact to open panicles of few to many flowers. Flowers are showy and sessile or with short glandular stalks; the calyx is 5-lobed, with the lobes long-pointed; the 5-lobed corolla is trumpet-shaped and white, pink, or reddish purple; the tube is about ½ in. long, and the lobes are spreading and rounded; there are 5 stamens. Fruits are ¼ in.–long capsules that contain few seeds.

Blooming Period
May–July.

Habitat
Tallgrass prairies, especially in limestone soil; E ¼.

Large populations of this wildflower can be truly stunning. Some of the best stands are seen on annually mowed prairies.

Blue phlox [*P. divaricata* L. subsp. *laphamii* (Wood) Wherry] is a woodland plant with light blue to lavender flowers. It occurs in the eastern quarter of the region.

Krameria lanceolata Torr.

Ratany

Krameriaceae
Ratany Family

Description
Ratany is a low perennial herb, with numerous spreading stems ½–3½ ft. long and a woody, branched rootstock. Leaves are alternate, simple, linear to oblong, up to ¾ in. long, and usually with a short brownish spine at the tip. Flowers arise from the bases of leaves on short stalks; they are orchidlike, with 4 or 5 prominent reddish or reddish brown sepals; there are 5 petals, the upper 3 red and the lower 2 thick and green; there are 4 stamens. Fruits* are small, woolly, and prickly and contain a single seed.

Blooming Period
May–July.

Habitat
Dry, rocky to gravelly or sandy shortgrass and mixed prairies; S ½.

The Ratany or Krameria Family is a small group of about 15 species restricted to the New World, mainly in dry regions. It is probably related most closely to the Milkwort Family.

Asclepias speciosa Torr.

Showy milkweed

Asclepiadaceae
Milkweed Family

Description

Showy milkweed is a stout, erect, perennial herb 1½–3½ ft. tall. Stems are densely hairy and mostly unbranched and contain copious milky sap. Leaves are opposite, simple, fleshy, hairy, 3–8 in. long, 1–5 in. wide, and broadly lance-shaped to egg-shaped, with short stalks. Inflorescences are few to several spherical umbels situated at the bases of upper leaves. Each umbel contains 10–40 woolly flowers, which are 5-parted with greenish sepals, rose or purple-rose petals, pale rose to creamy pink hoods, and prominent pink horns. Fruits* are large woolly pods up to 5 in. long with blunt spines and contain numerous seeds,* each tipped with a tuft of long white or tan hairs.

Blooming Period

May–August.

Habitat

Moist sandy, loamy, or rocky soils of most prairie types and along rivers, streams, and ponds; W ¾.

Common milkweed (*A. syriaca* L.) occurs throughout the eastern half of our region and is distinguished from the showy milkweed by its shorter hoods and knobby fruits. Sullivant milkweed, or smooth milkweed (*A. sullivantii* Engelm.), has hairless leaves and is restricted to tallgrass prairies in the northeastern quarter of the region.

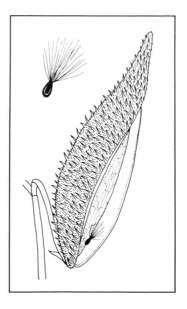

Coryphantha vivipara (Nutt.) Britt. & Rose

Pincushion cactus

Cactaceae
Cactus Family

Blooming Period
May–August.

Habitat
Mixed and shortgrass prairies, frequently on dry, rocky to sandy slopes and uplands; W ½.

This beautiful little plant can form large populations on some shortgrass prairies. Missouri coryphantha [*C. missouriensis* (Sweet) Britt. & Rose] occurs primarily in the eastern half of our region on rocky tallgrass and mixed prairies. It has pale-yellow or greenish flowers, red fruits, and few or no central spines.

Description
Pincushion cactus is rounded or short-cylindrical, grows up to 4 in. tall, and sometimes forms low mounds of many plants. Stems are green and covered with small bumps about ¼ in. in diameter; the top of each bump has a woolly mass of minute barbed hairs, a central group of 12–40 whitish spines,* and 3–4 reddish spines projecting outward. Leaves are absent. The showy dark-pink to reddish-purple flowers are 1 to several at the ends of stems, funnel-shaped, and 1–1½ in. long; the numerous stamens have yellow anthers and reddish filaments. Fruits* are green oblong berries 1 in. long and contain small brown seeds.

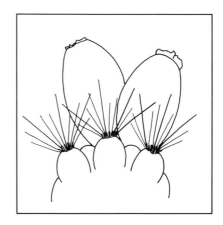

Hesperis matronalis L.

Dame's rocket

Brassicaceae
Mustard Family

Blooming Period
May–August.

Habitat
Roadsides, thickets, open woods, disturbed sites, and abandoned farmsteads; scattered over N ½ but less common in W.

This attractive mustard was introduced as an ornamental from Europe. It is now widely distributed throughout much of the eastern United States.

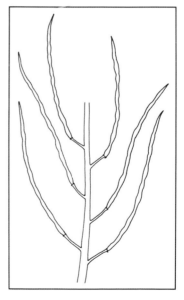

Description
Dame's rocket is an erect, hairy, biennial or perennial herb 1½–3½ ft. tall. Stems are often branched above. Leaves are alternate, simple, short-stalked to sessile, lance-shaped to nearly egg-shaped, 1–6 in. long, and ¼–1 in. wide, with toothed margins. Inflorescences are showy, many-flowered, terminal racemes. Flowers are 4-parted and fragrant; petals are reddish pink to bluish purple or rarely white and up to 1 in. long; there are 6 stamens, 4 of them long and 2 short. Fruits* are spreading, slender, dry, 2–6 in.–long pods that contain many angular, reddish brown, spindle-shaped seeds.

Rosa arkansana Porter

Prairie wild rose

Rosaceae
Rose Family

Description
Prairie wild rose is a subshrub that grows up to 3 ft. tall, although in mowed areas it behaves as a perennial herb that grows ¼–1½ ft. tall. Stems are 1 to several and branched and bear few to many slender, straight, unequal prickles; the twigs are reddish brown. Leaves are alternate, stalked, smooth to hairy and sometimes glandular, and odd-pinnately compound, with 7–11 egg-shaped to elliptic toothed leaflets ½–2½ in. long and ½–1½ in. wide. Inflorescences are showy few-flowered clusters at the ends of new stems. Sepals are 5, up to ¼ in. long, and glandular; the 5 pink, rose, or white petals are ½–1½ in. long; stamens are yellow and numerous. Fruits* are 15–30 plump long-hairy achenes contained in a bright red spherical hip about ½ in. in diameter, with the dried sepals attached.

Blooming Period
May–August.

Habitat
Most prairie types, open woods, thickets, fencerows, and roadsides; N ½ and infrequent in S.

The rose hip is a fleshy cup or vessel formed largely of calyx tissue. It contains the true fruits—the achenes—each of which develops from a separate pistil.
   Climbing prairie rose (*R. setigera* Michx.) is taller than the prairie wild rose, with 3–5 leaflets, hooked prickles, and pink petals; it occurs in similar habitats in the eastern quarter of the region. Multiflora rose (*R. multiflora* Thunb.) was introduced from Asia and occasionally becomes a serious weed in pastures and woodlands in the eastern third of the region. It has white 1 in.–wide flowers borne in dense panicles.

Carduus nutans L.

Musk thistle,
Nodding thistle

Asteraceae
Sunflower Family

Description
Musk thistle is a coarse, spiny, biennial herb 1–8 ft. tall and develops a large spiny rosette of leaves in the first year. Stems are typically multi-branched, with spiny wings running down from the leaf bases. Leaves are alternate, sessile, simple, lance-shaped to elliptic, 2–12 in. long, 1–4 in. wide, and usually with

deep lobes. The heads are solitary at the ends of branches, 1½–3 in. across, and usually nodding. Bracts of the heads are triangular and spreading or recurved, each bearing a strong spine at the tip; ray florets are absent; disk florets are reddish to reddish purple. Fruits are small angular achenes with a tuft of simple bristles at the tip.

Blooming Period
May–September.

Habitat
A variety of disturbed sites, including fields, pastures, roadsides, and waste ground, and occasionally tallgrass prairies; E ½.

Musk thistle is an aggressive, persistent weed capable of forming dense, impenetrable colonies. Introduced from Europe, it invaded the northern part of our region in the 1930s and is now well established throughout the eastern half. The species is legally noxious in some states.

The dried fruiting heads resemble strawflowers and can be used in arrangements. The spiny stems can be replaced with wire.

Ipomoea leptophylla Torr.

Bush morning-glory

Convolvulaceae
Morning Glory Family

Description

Bush morning-glory is a bushy, smooth, perennial herb 1–5 ft. tall and often as wide, arising from a woody, sometimes massive root. Stems are several to many, spreading to erect, and branched. Leaves* are alternate, simple, short-stalked, linear to narrowly lance-shaped, 1–6 in. long, and mostly less than ¼ in. wide. Inflorescences are few-flowered clusters on stalks that grow up to 4 in. long and arise from the bases of leaves. The calyx is 5-lobed and the sepals are unequal; the corolla is funnel-shaped, up to 3 in. wide, slightly 5-angled, pleated, and reddish pink to reddish purple, with a fringed margin; stamens are 5. Fruits* are ½ in.–long, smooth, egg-shaped capsules containing 1–4 brown densely short-hairy seeds.

Blooming Period

May–September.

Habitat

Sandy to gravelly mixed, shortgrass, and sandsage prairies, roadsides, and disturbed sites; W ⅔.

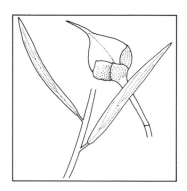

Coronilla varia L.

Crown vetch

Fabaceae
Bean Family

Description
Crown vetch is a spreading or ascending, smooth, perennial herb, arising from a taproot. Stems are branched and 1–4 ft. long and often form dense tangled mats on the ground. Leaves are alternate, stalked below to sessile above, 2–5 in. long, and odd-pinnately compound, with 9–25 egg-shaped leaflets about ½ in. long. Inflorescences are spherical umbels arising from the bases of leaves and bearing 5–20 flowers. The calyx is 5-lobed, with the upper 2 lobes longer than the lower ones; petals are pink or white; the 10 stamens are in 2 groups, 9 fused by their filaments and 1 free. Fruits are 1–2 in.–long cylindrical legumes that contain 3–12 smooth reddish brown seeds.

Blooming Period
May–September.

Habitat
Roadside banks, fields, pastures, and disturbed sites; E ½.

Crown vetch is frequently planted along highways and on exposed slopes to control soil erosion. It is also used as an ornamental. The species is native to Europe.

Trifolium pratense L.

Red clover

Fabaceae
Bean Family

rarely white; there are 10 stamens, 9 joined by their filaments and 1 free. Fruits are short egg-shaped legumes containing 1–2 small brownish seeds.

Blooming Period
May–September.

Habitat
Fields, pastures, roadsides, tallgrass prairies, and waste places; E ½ and infrequent in W.

Red clover is a valuable hay and pasture plant that was introduced from Eurasia. It is found on many native hay meadows in the region. The sweet flowers are edible, and the leaves (sometimes combined with the flowers) have been used to make a medicinal tea.

Description
Red clover is a tufted, short-lived, perennial herb 1–3 ft. tall, with a deep taproot. Stems are several to many, nearly smooth to appressed-hairy, and branched. Leaves* are alternate, long-stalked below to sessile above, and palmately compound, with 3 elliptic to egg-shaped, entire to finely toothed, soft-hairy leaflets ¾–2½ in. long and ½–1½ in. wide and bearing a light green crescent on the upper surface. Inflorescences are dense, rounded, sessile or short-stalked heads at the ends of branches. Flowers number 25–80 and are 5-parted and about ¾ in. long; the petals are pink or reddish,

Gaura parviflora Dougl.

Velvety gaura

Onagraceae
Evening Primrose Family

branched, sticky, terminal spikes. Flowers are sessile and with a short slender floral tube atop the ovary; sepals are 4 and reflexed; petals are 4, reddish pink to red, and less than ⅛ in. long; the 8 stamens are yellow to red. Fruits* are smooth or short-hairy spindle-shaped capsules containing 3–4 reddish brown seeds.

Blooming Period
May–October.

Habitat
All prairie types, open woods, pastures, roadsides, and disturbed sites; throughout region.

Description
Velvety gaura is an erect, densely glandular-hairy, annual herb 1–10 ft. tall. Stems are single and mostly unbranched and arise from a stout taproot. Leaves are alternate, simple, sessile, lance-elliptic to egg-shaped, 1–5 in. long, and ¼–2 in. wide, with somewhat wavy-toothed margins; lower stem leaves usually are absent on flowering plants. Inflorescences are

Mirabilis nyctaginea (Michx.) MacM.

Wild four-o'clock

Nyctaginaceae
Four-O'Clock Family

Description
Wild four-o'clock is an erect, smooth or very sparingly hairy, slightly waxy, perennial herb 1–4 ft. tall, with a thick fleshy taproot. Stems are 1 to several and branched, with swollen nodes. Leaves are opposite, simple, stalked, entire, lance-shaped to heart-shaped or triangular, 2–5 in. long, and 1–4 in. wide. Inflorescences are few-flowered, umbel-like clusters at the ends of branches, each with a 5-lobed leafy skirt below the flower; the 5-lobed petal-like calyx is rose to reddish purple, bell-shaped to funnel-shaped, and about ½ in. wide; petals are absent; stamens are 3–5. Fruits are short, hard, cylindrical, dark, 5-ribbed, and bumpy and contain a single brownish seed.

Blooming Period
May–October.

Habitat
Disturbed sites, including prairies, pastures, fields, roadsides, open woods, and waste places; throughout region but infrequently in SW ¼.

As indicated by the common name, flowers tend to open in the late afternoon.

Nine other species occur in the region. Narrowleaf four-o'clock [*M. linearis* (Pursh) Heimerl.] occurs throughout the region and is common on some prairies. It has linear leaves usually less than ⅛ in. wide, smooth stems, and hairy wrinkled fruits. White four-o'clock [*M. albida* (Walt.) Heimerl.] can be distinguished by its leaves up to 1 in. wide, white or pinkish flowers, and warty fruits.

Sabatia campestris Nutt.

Prairie rose gentian

Gentianaceae
Gentian Family

Description
Prairie rose gentian is a smooth, erect, annual herb ¼–1 ft. tall, with a taproot. Stems are slender, angular, and unbranched below the inflorescence. Leaves are opposite, simple, sessile and clasping, narrowly egg-shaped, ¼–1 in. long, and less than ½ in. wide, with entire margins. Inflorescences are open, few-flowered, terminal clusters on long stalks. The calyx is 5-lobed, with prominent ribs; the corolla is 5-lobed and wheel-shaped, with the lobes spreading and up to 1 in. long and bright pink with a pale throat; stamens are 5 and bright yellow. Fruits are smooth cylindrical to egg-shaped capsules that contain many tiny, pitted, gray seeds.

Blooming Period
June–July.

Habitat
Tallgrass prairies, pastures, roadsides, and disturbed sites; SE ¼.

Echinacea angustifolia DC.

Narrow-leaf purple coneflower,
Black sampson echinacea

Asteraceae
Sunflower Family

Description
Narrow-leaf purple coneflower is an erect, coarsely hairy, perennial herb ½–2 ft. tall, arising from a woody taproot. Stems are 1 to several and sometimes branched. Leaves are alternate, simple, stalked below to sessile above, narrowly lance-shaped to egg-shaped, 2–12 in. long, and ½–1½ in. wide, with entire margins. Inflorescences are terminal heads, 1½—3 in. wide, and produced at the ends of long stalks. Bracts on the heads are lance-shaped; ray florets are 1–1½ in. long, spreading or drooping, light pink to pale purple; disk florets are 5-lobed, numerous, and brownish purple and situated among abundant stiff bracts* that are most obvious when the plant is fruiting. Fruits are small, dark, hairless, 4-angled achenes with a crown of short teeth at the tip.

Blooming Period
June–July.

Habitat
Nearly all prairies on rocky slopes and uplands; W ⅘.

Pale coneflower [*E. pallida* (Nutt.) Nutt.] occurs on rocky tallgrass prairies in the eastern quarter of our region; it has ray florets that are mostly 1½–3 in. long. Yellow echinacea (*E. atrorubens* Nutt.) is encountered in a narrow north-south band in the eastern quarter of the region. It has short dark purple ray florets that curve under the head, often touching the flowering stalk.

Populations of *Echinacea* are in danger of being overcollected for their roots, which are purchased by pharmaceutical companies and used in drug formulations.

Cirsium undulatum (Nutt.) Spreng.

Wavy-leaf thistle

Asteraceae
Sunflower Family

Description
Wavy-leaf thistle is an erect, densely white-woolly, spiny, perennial herb 1–5 ft. tall, with a short, stout taproot. Stems are grooved and sometimes branched above. Leaves are alternate, simple, lance-shaped to elliptic, often pinnately lobed, 4–12 in. long, and 1–4 in. wide, with wavy margins bearing yellowish spines. Heads are single, 1–2 in. wide,

and at the ends of the branches. Bracts on the heads each usually bear a short, spreading spine at the tip; ray florets are absent; disk florets are pale pink to purple or occasionally white. Fruits are small brownish achenes with white, feathery bristles at the tip.

Blooming Period
June–August.

Habitat
All types of prairies, pastures, roadsides, and disturbed sites; throughout region.

Yellowspine thistle (*C. ochrocentrum* A. Gray) occurs in the western two-thirds of the region on dry, sandy to gravelly, . shortgrass and mixed prairies. It is also white-woolly but has leafy wings on the stems that extend down from the leaf bases. Bull thistle [*C. vulgare* (Savi) Ten.], a weedy biennial with short appressed prickles on the upper leaf surfaces, is also found in the eastern half of the region. Dried fruiting heads of thistles are an attractive beige, useful in winter arrangements.

Ratibida tagetes (James) Barnh.

Short-ray prairie coneflower

Asteraceae
Sunflower Family

Description

Short-ray prairie coneflower is an erect, leafy, appressed-hairy, somewhat gland-dotted, perennial herb ½–1½ ft. tall, with a stout taproot. Stems are 1 to several and multi-branched. Leaves are alternate and short-stalked; the lower ones are 1–5 in. long, lance-shaped, and entire or 1–2 times pinnately divided; upper leaves are more deeply divided, with 3–5 linear segments. Inflorescences are mostly solitary spherical heads up to ½ in. long on short stalks and often closely clustered. Ray florets are 5–10, yellow to purplish brown, about ¼ in. long, and drooping; disk florets are purplish brown and abundant. Fruits are short, gray, flattened, winged, mostly smooth achenes with a crown of thick toothlike scales at the tip.

Blooming Period
June–September.

Habitat
Dry, rocky, mixed and shortgrass prairies; W ½.

Asclepias incarnata L.

Swamp milkweeed

Asclepiadaceae
Milkweed Family

region except SW ¼ and most abundant in E.

The species name, "*incarnata*," is Latin for "flesh," an allusion to the flesh-colored flowers. Milkweeds have potential economic value. The seed hairs can be used to stuff insulated items such as sleeping bags. Stem fibers were used by several Indian tribes to make rope and fishing nets.

Description

Swamp milkweed is an erect perennial herb 1½–8 ft. tall. Stems are often hairy and sometimes branched and contain milky sap. Leaves are mostly opposite, simple, linear to egg-shaped, 2–6 in. long, and ½–1½ in. wide, with short stalks. Inflorescences are few to several umbels up to 3 in. across arising from the ends of the stems. Each umbel bears 10–40 hairy, pale to deep pink flowers, which are 5-parted and bear whitish or pinkish hoods and white horns. Fruits* are narrow, smooth to sparsely hairy pods containing abundant seeds, each with a tuft of white hairs at the tip.

Blooming Period
June–September.

Habitat
Along rivers, streams, ponds, lakes, marshes, and wet prairies; throughout

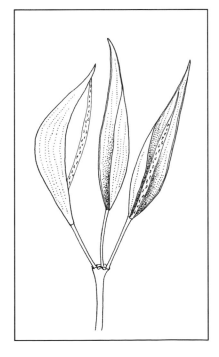

Desmodium illinoense A. Gray

Illinois tickclover

Fabaceae
Bean Family

Description
Illinois tickclover is a hairy, erect, perennial herb that grows up to 6 ft. tall, with a slender taproot. Stems are mostly unbranched and covered with a mixture of tiny glandular and hook-shaped hairs. Leaves are alternate, distinctly stalked with 3 lance-shaped to egg-shaped leaflets, and 2½–6 in. long. Inflorescences are terminal racemes with thick, hairy, mostly unbranched, central stalks. Flowers are 5-parted; the petals are mostly pink to purplish, the upper one prominent and often with a purplish spot near the base; stamens are 10, with 9 joined by their filaments and 1 free. Fruits* are flattened, hairy, sticky legumes, constricted between each of the 2–8 smooth brown seeds.

Blooming Period
June–September.

Habitat
Tallgrass prairies, roadsides, and infrequently in open wooded areas; E ½.

Tickclovers are well known to hikers, hunters, nature lovers, and dog owners for fruits that cling to clothing and fur like small ticks. This adaptation enables the plants to disperse seeds widely.
   Hoary tickclover [*D. canescens* (L.) DC.] occurs in open woods and thickets and along stream banks in the eastern half of the region. It has long, spreading hairs in the inflorescences, multibranched stems, and angular fruit segments.

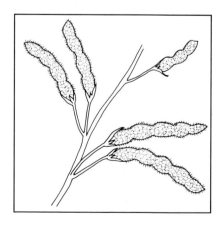

Desmodium sessilifolium (Torr.) T. & G.

Sessile-leaved tickclover

Fabaceae
Bean Family

hairy with tiny hooked hairs. Leaves are alternate, short-stalked or sessile with 3 narrowly elliptic to narrowly lance-shaped leaflets, and 2–4 in. long. Inflorescences are hairy, usually branched, terminal racemes. Flowers are numerous, small, and 5-parted; petals are variable in color and may be pink, pale lavender, yellowish white, or white; stamens are 10, with 9 joined by their filaments and 1 free. Fruits are flattened, hairy, sticky, legumes constricted between each of the 2–4 smooth brownish seeds.

Blooming Period
July–September.

Habitat
Tallgrass prairies, open woods, and roadsides, often in shallow rocky soil; E ½.

Description
Sessile-leaved tickclover is an erect perennial that grows up to 4½ ft. tall, with a stout taproot. Stems are 1 to several, mostly unbranched, ribbed, and densely

Large-flowered tickclover [D. glutinosum (Muhl. ex Willd.) Wood] is a woodland species with leaves clustered halfway up the stem and all stamens joined by their filaments in a single group.

Polygonum amphibium L.

Water smartweed

Polygonaceae
Buckwheat Family

Description

Water smartweed is a floating, creeping, or erect, smooth or appressed-hairy, colonial, perennial herb that grows up to 5 ft. tall. Stems are several to many and branched and arise from dark branched rhizomes. Leaves are alternate, simple, stalked, mostly lance-shaped, 1–10 in. long, and ½–2½ in. wide, with entire or wavy margins; prominent stipules wrap around the stem at the bases of leaves and inflorescences. Inflorescences are 1–2 erect, terminal, spikelike racemes ½–4 in. long. Sepals are 5, petal-like, pink to rose, and about ⅛ in. long; petals are absent; stamens are 8. Fruits are small, shiny, reddish brown, lens-shaped achenes.

Blooming Period

June–September.

Habitat

Quiet, shallow water, muddy or sandy shores, ditches, and roadsides; throughout region but less common in W.

This widespread species is treated as *P. coccineum* Muhl. in many floras and wildflower books. Plants are quite variable and colonize habitats ranging from shallow permanent water to seasonally wet depressions. The name "smartweed" refers to the strong acid juice in these plants.

Polygonum bicorne Raf.

Pink smartweed

Polygonaceae
Buckwheat Family

up to 6 in. long and 1 in. wide; prominent stipules wrap around the stem at the base of leaves and inflorescences. Inflorescences are erect spike-like racemes ½–2½ in. long on long stalks arising from the bases of leaves or the ends of branches. Sepals are 5, petal-like, pink, and about ⅛ in. long; petals are absent; stamens are 5. Fruits are small, brown, lens-shaped achenes.

Blooming Period
July–October.

Habitat
Damp or wet sites along rivers, streams, ponds, marshes, and ditches; throughout region.

Description
Pink smartweed is an erect, gland-dotted, annual or short-lived perennial herb that grows up to 6 ft. tall and has fibrous roots. Stems are several to many, multi-branched, and usually glandular-hairy above. Leaves are alternate, simple, stalked, entire, mostly lance-shaped, and

Some plants have stamens longer than the sepals and short styles; others have short stamens and styles longer than the sepals. This condition occurs in numerous groups of flowering plants and promotes cross-pollination.

Pennsylvania smartweed (*P. pensylvanicum* L.) is similar to pink smartweed but has pink or white sepals and stamens and styles about equal in length.

Polygonum lapathifolium L.

Pale smartweed

Polygonaceae
Buckwheat Family

and inflorescences. Inflorescences are numerous, dense, drooping racemes up to 3 in. long on stalks arising from the ends of branches. Sepals are 5, petal-like, pink, white, or green, about ⅛ in. long, and with 3 veins; stamens are 5. Fruits are small, reddish brown, lens-shaped achenes.

Blooming Period
July–October.

Habitat
Damp or wet disturbed sites, including fields, ponds, and ditches; throughout region.

Description
Pale smartweed is an erect or ascending, smooth to somewhat hairy, annual herb 2–7 ft. tall, with a taproot. Stems are single, usually branched, and sometimes with the lower branches on the ground and rooted at the nodes. Leaves are alternate, simple, entire, stalked, gland-dotted on the lower surface, lance-shaped to elliptic, 2–8 in. long, and ½–1½ in. wide; prominent stipules* wrap around the stem at the bases of leaves

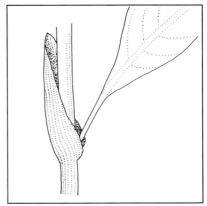

Apios americana Medic.

Groundnut,
American potato bean

Fabaceae
Bean Family

brown on the front, the other 4 petals are reddish brown; there are 10 stamens, 9 joined by their filaments and 1 free. Fruits* are linear legumes 2–5 in. long that contain 2–12 brown wrinkled seeds.

Blooming Period
July–September.

Habitat
Moist woods, thickets, stream and river-banks, and prairie ravines; E ½ and infrequent in W.

The tubers of groundnut are edible and were a valuable source of food for many Indian tribes and early European settlers. The species has been considered as a potential commercial root crop.

Description
Groundnut is a trailing or climbing, smooth to hairy, perennial vine with slender rhizomes bearing tuberlike thickenings.* Stems are several to many, branched, and 3–20 ft. long. Leaves are alternate, stalked, and odd-pinnate, with 5–7 lance-shaped to egg-shaped, 1–4 in.–long, entire leaflets. Inflorescences are open to compact racemes 1–8 in. long on short stalks arising from the bases of leaves. Flowers are 5-parted and about ½ in. long; the prominent upper petal is whitish on the back and reddish

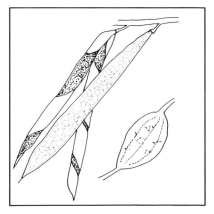

Ammannia coccinea Rottb.

Purple toothcup

Lythraceae
Loosestrife Family

Blooming Period
July–October.

Habitat
Wet sites along rivers, streams, lakes, and ponds; E ¾.

Two other toothcups occur in our area. Lavender toothcup (*A. robusta* Heer & Regel) has sessile flowers and pale lavender petals. Earleaf toothcup (*A. auriculata* Willd.) is more slender than purple toothcup and has numerous flowers with long stalks and rose-purple petals. Purple toothcup is believed to have evolved from the past hybridization of these two species.

Description
Purple toothcup is a weak to robust, erect, smooth, annual herb that grows up to 3 ft. tall but generally is much shorter. Stems are multi-branched, fleshy, and often reddish. Leaves are opposite, simple, sessile, fleshy, lance-shaped to oblong, and up to 3 in. long and ½ in. wide. Flowers are in clusters of 3–10 at the bases of leaves. Each small flower is 4-parted with short green sepals and dark pink to rose petals that fall off readily; 4–8 deep yellow anthers project above the petals. Fruits* are small spherical capsules filled with abundant tiny seeds.

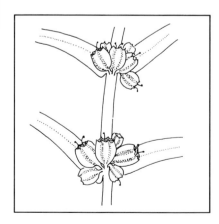

Aster subulatus Michx. var. *ligulatus* Shinners

Saltmarsh aster

Asteraceae
Sunflower Family

Description
Saltmarsh aster is an erect, smooth, annual herb ¼–3 ft. tall, with a short taproot. Stems are single but multi-branched above. Leaves are alternate, simple, sessile, and slightly clasping, linear to narrowly lance-shaped, ¼–4 in. long, and ¼–1 in. wide, with entire or scarcely toothed margins. Inflorescences are open, spreading panicles of few to many heads borne near the ends of branches. Bracts on the heads are linear; ray florets are 15–30, pink to light purple or white, and less than ¼ in. long; disk florets are yellow. Fruits are small, short-hairy, brown achenes tipped with abundant slender white bristles.

Blooming Period
August–October.

Habitat
Low, wet or drying sites, including ditches, fields, and salt marshes; S ½ and C ⅓ of N ½.

Lobelia cardinalis L.

Cardinal flower

Campanulaceae
Bellflower Family

Description

Cardinal flower is an erect, smooth, perennial herb ½–4 ft. tall, with milky sap and fibrous roots. Stems are mostly single, unbranched, and leafy. Leaves are alternate, simple, short-stalked to sessile, gradually reduced up the stem, lance-shaped to elliptic, 2–8 in. long, and ¼–2 in. wide, with toothed margins. Inflorescences are showy, somewhat dense terminal racemes that grow up to 2 ft. long. The brilliant red flowers are 5-lobed and 1–2 in. long; the corolla is 2-lipped, with the lower 3 lobes spreading and the upper 2 erect and shorter; stamens are 5, with the reddish filaments and gray anthers united and forming a tube around

the style. Fruits* are cup-shaped capsules that contain numerous tiny brownish seeds.

Blooming Period
August–October.

Habitat
Open wet ground on prairies, in woods and marshes, and along rivers and streams; throughout region but infrequent in W ⅓.

This stunning species ranks among the most beautiful of our Great Plains wildflowers. Cultivated varieties are available for gardens.

Blue cardinal flower (*L. siphilitica* L.) has large pale blue to blue flowers. It occurs in the same habitats as cardinal flower but is found predominantly in the northeastern half of the region.

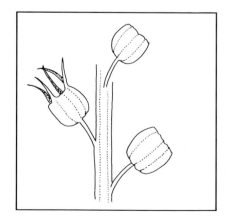

Blue, Lavender, Violet, or Purple

Viola rafinesquii Greene

Johnny-jump-up,
Wild pansy

Violaceae
Violet Family

Description

Johnny-jump-up is a slender, erect, smooth to short-hairy, annual herb 1½– 8 in. tall, with a taproot. Stems are single and usually branched from the base. Leaves are alternate, simple, stalked, ovate to kidney-shaped, ¼–1 in. long, and ¼–½ in. wide, with shallowly toothed margins; prominent stipules* at the bases of leaves are leafy and palmately divided. Flowers are solitary on stalks ½–1 in. long and arise from the bases of leaves, especially toward the ends of branches; sepals are 5 and broadly lance-shaped; petals are 5, bluish white to blue with purplish lines within,

and over ¼ in. long—the 2 lateral ones are bearded and the lower 1 is yellowish at the base and short-spurred; the 5 stamens surround the style. Fruits are egg-shaped yellowish capsules that contain numerous small smooth seeds.

Blooming Period
March–June.

Habitat
Tallgrass and mixed prairies, open woods, roadsides, pastures, and waste areas; E ½.

Johnny-jump-up looks like a miniature version of the garden pansy (*V. tricolor* L.). Dense patches in open, disturbed sites can be quite attractive. The common name refers to the quick growth of this plant in the spring.

Anemone caroliniana Walt.

Carolina anemone

Ranunculaceae
Buttercup Family

Description
Carolina anemone is a delicate perennial herb 3–12 in. tall. Stems are slender and smooth below but densely hairy above and arise from tuberous thickenings along a slender rhizome. Basal leaves are smooth to sparingly hairy, 1–6 in. long and 1–2 in. wide, dissected into 3-lobed segments and have a prominent stalk; stem leaves are mostly sessile and dissected into narrow segments. Flowers are solitary, ½–1½ in. across, with 10–30 lavender, white, or violet petal-like sepals; true petals are absent; stamens and pistils are bright yellow. Fruits* are elongate clusters of small woolly achenes.

Blooming Period
April–May.

Habitat
Tallgrass, mixed, and sand prairies in a variety of soil types; E ½.

This beautiful flower is a harbinger of spring. It is most easily located where the vegetation is short or sparse. The flowers close at night and on cloudy days.

This genus includes some 150 species worldwide. *Anemone* is derived from a Greek root meaning "of the wind"— hence the common name "windflowers."

Astragalus crassicarpus Nutt.

Ground-plum

Fabaceae
Bean Family

Description
Ground-plum is a low perennial herb, with a thick woody taproot. Stems are several to many, spreading, ½–2 ft. long, and slightly to moderately hairy. Leaves are alternate, spreading-hairy, 2–6 in. long, ½–¾ in. wide, and odd-pinnately compound, with 7–13 pairs of elliptic leaflets. Inflorescences are short rounded to cylindrical racemes of 5–25 flowers. Flowers are 5-parted; petals are variable in color but frequently purple, violet, bluish, or pinkish red; the upper petal is usually prominent; there are 10 stamens, 9 joined by their filaments and 1 free. Fruits are plump fleshy legumes that become dry and woody with age; they contain numerous small seeds.

Blooming Period
March–June.

Habitat
All prairie types and occasionally in open, rocky woods and disturbed sites; throughout region.

The fruits of this widespread and common prairie legume are edible and taste like pea pods. Rodents are fond of the fruits, so toothmarks are not unusual on legumes in the field.

A similar species, Platte River milk-vetch (*A. plattensis* Nutt. ex T. & G.), can be distinguished by its hairy fruits. It is found throughout much of the western two-thirds of our region.

Astragalus missouriensis Nutt.

Missouri milk-vetch

Fabaceae
Bean Family

Description

Missouri milk-vetch is a low, tufted or spreading, perennial herb covered with dense, minute, picklike hairs that give the plant a grayish or silvery appearance. Stems are ½–5½ in. long and few to several, arising from a woody taproot. Leaves are alternate, 1–5 in. long, ¼–¾ in. wide, and odd-pinnately compound, with 3–10 pairs of elliptic leaflets. Inflorescences are short racemes of 3–15 flowers on stalks roughly as long as the leaves. The corolla is purple to bluish, and the upper petal usually has a whitish center; 9 of the 10 stamens are joined by their filaments. Fruits* are hairy boat-shaped legumes containing small brown seeds.

Blooming Period

March–July.

Habitat

Most prairie types, especially on rocky limestone soils; W ⅔.

Astragalus mollissimus Torr.

Woolly locoweed

Fabaceae
Bean Family

Description
Woolly locoweed is a low, tufted, perennial herb densely covered with silvery hairs. Stems are 1 to several, ¾–6 in. tall, and spreading to erect. Leaves are alternate, 2½–10 in. long, ½–1½ in. wide, and odd-pinnately compound, with 7–15 pairs of oval leaflets. Inflorescences are short to long racemes of 10–40 flowers produced at the ends of long stalks. The corolla is yellowish purple to reddish purple with a prominent upper petal. Fruits are egg-shaped legumes that are usually smooth and contain small brownish seeds.

Blooming Period
April–June.

Habitat
Mixed, shortgrass, and sandsage prairies; W ½.

Several of the Great Plains members of this genus, including woolly locoweed, are toxic to livestock. Members of the genus *Oxytropis,* also known as "locoweeds," resemble species of *Astragalus.* However, the two united petals in *Oxytropis* are beaked or pointed, whereas in *Astragalus,* they are blunt or rounded.

Baptisia australis (L.) R. Br. var. *minor* (Lehm.) S. Wats.

Blue false indigo

Fabaceae
Bean Family

Description
Blue false indigo is a robust, smooth, perennial herb 1½–4 ft. tall, with a waxy appearance. Stems are multi-branched above. Leaves are alternate and stalked, with 3 elliptic or wedge-shaped leaflets 1–3 in. long and ¼–1 in. wide. Inflorescences are prominent erect racemes that grow up to 1½ ft. long and project above the leaves. The large showy flowers are pale to dark purplish blue with a prominent upper petal; the 10 stamens are separate. Fruits* are inflated beaked legumes 1–2½ in. long and contain small dark seeds.

Blooming Period
April–June.

Habitat
Tallgrass and mixed prairies, especially in limestone and clay soils; SE ½.

The common name distinguishes this species from the true indigo (*Indigofera tinctoria* L.) used to make blue dye. Unfortunately, the beautiful flowers of blue false indigo turn black shortly after they are picked. However, the fruits can be used in dried arrangements.

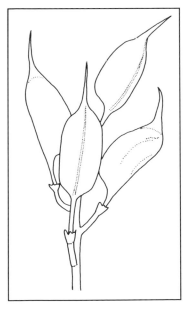

Viola pedatifida G. Don

Prairie violet,
Larkspur violet

Violaceae
Violet Family

are bearded and the lowest has a short spur; the 5 yellowish stamens surround the style. Fruits are smooth egg-shaped capsules containing many yellowish seeds.

Blooming Period
April–June and infrequently again in August–September.

Habitat
Tallgrass prairies and occasionally open woods; E ⅓.

This species hybridizes with blue prairie violet (*V. pratincola* Greene) and downy blue violet (*V. sororia* Willd.), both of which occur on tallgrass prairies and open woods in the eastern quarter of our region. Blue prairie violet also inhabits mixed and shortgrass prairies in the western two-thirds of the region. It has leaf blades that are kidney-shaped to heart-shaped and smooth, and the spurred petal lacks hairs. It is treated as *V. missouriensis* Greene in many earlier works.

Description
Prairie violet is a low, stemless, mostly smooth, perennial herb, with a short stout rootstock. Leaves are few to many and long-stalked, 1–3 in. long, 1–4 in. wide, and shallowly to deeply palmately 3-lobed, with the segments occasionally divided again into 3–7 linear to lance-shaped parts that sometimes bear teeth. Flowers are solitary on 1 to several 2–8 in.–long naked stalks; sepals are 5 and broadly lance-shaped; the 5 petals are purple and ½–¾ in. long—the lower 3

Chorispora tenella (Pall.) DC.

Blue mustard

Brassicaceae
Mustard Family

Description

Blue mustard is an erect or spreading winter annual, with scattered glandular hairs,* especially toward the top of the plant. Stems are usually branched and ½–1½ ft. tall. Leaves are alternate, simple, stalked, mostly lance-shaped, 1–4 in. long, and ½—1 in. wide, with entire to wavy-toothed margins. Inflorescences are spikes of 10–30 bluish to bluish purple flowers. The calyx and corolla are 4-parted, and there are 4 long and 2 short stamens. Fruits are long, slender, upward-curved capsules 1–2 in. long, with a small seedless beak at the tip; seeds are small, rounded, and numerous.

Blooming Period
April–July

Habitat
Disturbed sites, including fields, pastures, roadsides, lawns, and waste areas; scattered throughout region but apparently less common in S ½.

Blue mustard was introduced to North America from Asia and is a well-established weed in much of the United States, particularly the western states. Plants in the Great Plains frequently form dense blue carpets in the spring in cultivated fields, often in association with purple-flowered henbit (*Lamium amplexicaule* L.) and yellow-flowered treacle mustard (*Erysimum repandum* L.). Plants typically have a sweet-musty odor that is most obvious in large populations.

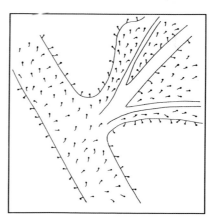

Penstemon buckleyi Penn.

Buckley's beardtongue,
Buckley's penstemon

Scrophulariaceae
Figwort Family

above, entire, spatula-shaped below to lance-shaped or egg-shaped above, 1–6 in. long, and ¼–1 in. wide. Inflorescences are narrow many-flowered panicles up to 20 in. long. The calyx is 5-lobed; the corolla is funnel-shaped, up to ¾ in. long, somewhat 2-lipped with 2 upper lobes and 3 lower lobes, and pale pink or lavender, with reddish lines within; the 5 stamens include a sterile one bearing yellow hairs along half its length. Fruits are woody egg-shaped capsules containing numerous small, angular, brown seeds.

Blooming Period
April–June.

Habitat
Sand and sandsage prairies and sandy habitats in mixed and shortgrass prairies; SW ½.

Description
Buckley's beardtongue is a stout, erect, smooth and waxy, perennial herb ½–3 ft. tall. Stems are 1 to several and unbranched. Leaves are opposite, simple, stalked below but sessile and clasping

Penstemon is a genus of nearly 300 species essentially restricted to North America. Most species are found in the western United States.

Penstemon grandiflorus Nutt.

Large beardtongue,
Shull-leaf beardtongue

Scrophulariaceae
Figwort Family

corolla is inflated, up to 2 in. long, distinctly 2-lipped, with 2 upper lobes and 3 lower lobes, and bluish lavender to pale blue, with faint reddish lines within; the 5 stamens include a sterile one that is bearded with yellow hairs at the tip. Fruits* are woody, egg-shaped capsules that contain numerous small, angular, brown seeds.

Blooming Period
April–July.

Habitat
Most prairie types in sandy to loamy soil; discontinuous over E ½ and essentially absent along E edge.

Description
Large beardtongue is a stout, erect, perennial herb 1½–4 ft. tall, with smooth waxy herbage. Stems are 1 to several and unbranched. Leaves are opposite, simple, stalked below but sessile and clasping above, entire, spatula-shaped below to egg-shaped above, 1–6 in. long, and ½–2 in. wide. Inflorescences are narrow panicles up to 16 in. long, with large showy flowers. The calyx is 5-lobed; the

Oxytropis lambertii Pursh

Purple locoweed

Fabaceae
Bean Family

aments and 1 free. Fruits are ¼–1 in.–long, cylindrical, tapered legumes containing few smooth brown seeds.

Blooming Period
April–August.

Habitat
Mixed and shortgrass prairies and open wooded slopes, especially on rocky eroded ground; W ¾.

Like many species of milk-vetch (*Astragalus*), this plant accumulates and stores selenium from the soil, thus making it toxic to livestock. White locoweed (*O. sericea* Nutt.) has simple hairs and white flowers; it occurs in the northwestern quarter of our region and infrequently southward.

Description
Purple locoweed is an erect, stemless, perennial herb, with a stout taproot, and is silky-hairy with minute picklike hairs.* Leaves are basal and odd-pinnate, with 7–19 linear to elliptic entire leaflets ¼–1½ in. long and less than ¼ in. wide. Inflorescences are showy racemes of 10–30 flowers on naked stalks 2–12 in. long and held above the leaves. Flowers are about ¾ in. long; the calyx is 5-lobed and silky-hairy; petals are blue to purple or rose, with the upper one prominent; stamens are 10, with 9 joined by their fil-

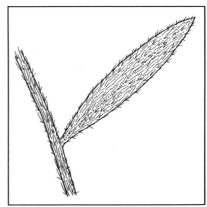

Scutellaria resinosa Torr.

Resinous skullcap

Lamiaceae
Mint Family

Description
Resinous skullcap is a low, stiff, short-hairy, resin-dotted, perennial herb ¼–1½ ft. tall, with a stout taproot. Stems are usually numerous and 4-angled. Leaves are opposite, simple, short-stalked or sessile, entire, slightly thickened, egg-shaped to broadly elliptic, ¼–¾ in. long, and mostly less than ¼ in. wide. Flowers are usually 2 per node in the upper half of the plant and arise from the bases of leaves on short stalks; the calyx is 2-parted, gland-dotted, and short-hairy, with a small swelling that is most obvious when the plant is fruiting; the corolla is 2-lipped and up to ¾ in. long—the lower lip is deep blue with white spreading lobes, and the upper lip is arched; the 4 stamens are hidden by the upper lip. Fruits are composed of 4 small, bumpy, black nutlets, each containing a single seed.

Blooming Period
April–August.

Habitat
Mixed and shortgrass prairies, especially in dry, rocky, limestone soil; C ⅓.

"Skullcap" is an allusion to the shape of the enlarged fruiting calyx. Small skullcap (*S. parvula* Michx.) is a low perennial with creeping, swollen rhizomes. Three varieties occur in the region, all in the eastern third. Mad-dog skullcap (*S. lateriflora* L.) is a smooth perennial up to 3 ft. tall bearing short, 1-sided racemes that arise from leaf bases. It is found on wet ground throughout the region but is most common in the northern half.

Tradescantia ohiensis Raf.

Ohio spiderwort

Commelinaceae
Spiderwort Family

Description

Ohio spiderwort is an erect, smooth, waxy, somewhat fleshy, perennial herb 1½–3½ ft. tall, with fleshy, fibrous roots. Stems are 1 to several, slender, and often branched. Leaves are alternate, simple, entire, sheathing the stem at the nodes, narrowly lance-shaped to linear, 4–14 in. long, and ¼–¾ in. wide. Inflorescences are solitary or few terminal clusters of 5–20 flowers, with smooth stalks and slender leaflike bracts at the base. Flowers are 3-parted; sepals are smooth, waxy, and sometimes tinged red; the petals are ½–¾ in. long, broadly egg-shaped, and usually blue but also lavender to rose; stamens are 6, with densely hairy filaments. Fruits are rounded capsules containing 2–6 seeds.

Blooming Period

April–August.

Habitat

Tallgrass and mixed prairies, open woods, and disturbed sites; SE ½.

Members of this genus were thought to cure spider bites.

Tradescantia occidentalis (Britt.) Smyth

Prairie spiderwort

Commelinaceae
Spiderwort Family

Description
Prairie spiderwort is an erect, smooth, waxy, somewhat fleshy, perennial herb ½–1½ ft. tall, with fleshy fibrous roots. Stems are 1 to several, stout, and often branched. Leaves are alternate, simple, entire, sheathing the stem at the nodes, narrowly lance-shaped to linear, 4–12 in. long, and ¼–½ in. wide. Inflorescences are solitary or few terminal clusters of 3–20 flowers, with glandular-hairy stalks and slender leaflike bracts at the base. Flowers are 3-parted; sepals are about ½ in. long, slightly purple, and smooth to glandular-hairy; the petals are ½–¾ in. long, broadly egg-shaped, and blue, rose, or purple; the 6 stamens have densely hairy filaments. Fruits are rounded capsules containing 2–6 flattened seeds.

Blooming Period
May–August.

Habitat
Nearly all prairie types but most common on sand and sandsage prairies; W ⅔.

Bracted spiderwort (*T. bracteata* Small) is barely distinguishable from the prairie spiderwort in parts of the region, most notably where their ranges overlap. The former is a sparingly branched plant with glandular and nonglandular hairs on the sepals and is found on prairies in the northeastern half of our region.

Quincula lobata (Torr.) Raf.

Purple ground cherry

Solanaceae
Nightshade Family

Description

Purple ground cherry is a low, rhizoma-tous, perennial herb that forms spreading mats up to several feet in diameter. Stems are multi-branched. Leaves are alternate, 1–4 in. long, ¼–1 in. wide, with wavy margins and short stalks. Flowers are solitary on slender upright stalks arising from the bases of leaves; the calyx is 5-lobed; the corolla is pale to dark purple or bluish purple, flat and rounded to slightly angular; the 5 yellow stamens alternate with small hairy bumps at the throat of the corolla. Fruits* are small, spherical, yellow-green berries enclosed by the enlarged bladderlike calyx.

Blooming Period
April–October.

Habitat
Open, dry, sandy to gravelly, shortgrass and mixed prairies, especially in disturbed sites; SW ⅔.

Amorpha fruticosa L.

False indigo

Fabaceae
Bean Family

hairy below and smooth above. Inflorescences are dense racemes of 50–150 flowers arising from the bases of upper leaves. Flowers have a single bluish to violet petal folded around the stamens and pistil. Fruits* are short, smooth or hairy, glandular legumes containing a single smooth brownish seed.

Blooming Period
May–June.

Habitat
Wet ground along rivers, streams, ponds, and ditches, and occasionally in open wet woods; E ¾.

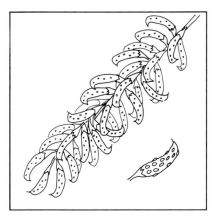

Description
False indigo is an erect shrub 3–10 ft. tall. Stems are 1 to several and often branched above. Leaves are alternate, elliptic, ½–2 in. long, ¼–1 in. wide, odd-pinnate, with stalks 1–1½ in. long and 4–15 pairs of elliptic leaflets bearing small glandular dots on their lower surfaces. Young leaves tend to be densely hairy, whereas older ones are mostly

Amorpha canescens Pursh

Lead plant

Fabaceae
Bean Family

Description
Lead plant is a short shrub 1–3 ft. tall, although in areas that are mowed, it behaves like a perennial herb. Stems are 1 to several, usually branched, and hairy except in older plants. Leaves are alternate, oblong, 1–2 in. long, ½–1½ in. wide, odd-pinnate with 5–20 pairs of oblong leaflets, and sparingly to densely hairy, with a grayish or whitish appearance. Inflorescences are dense racemes of 5–50 flowers arising from the bases of upper leaves. The small flowers have a single bluish to violet petal folded around the 10 stamens and the pistil. Fruits are short, hairy, glandular legumes containing a single smooth brownish seed.

Blooming Period
May–August.

Habitat
Nearly all prairie types and open woodlands; E ⅔ but infrequent in W.

Lead plant is a highly palatable range species and its presence on prairies is generally perceived to be the result of good land management. The claim that this species indicates the existence of lead deposits is only a superstition.

Psoralea cuspidata Pursh

Tall-bread scurf-pea

Fabaceae
Bean Family

Description
Tall-bread scurf-pea is a spreading or ascending, appressed-hairy, perennial herb ½–3 ft. tall, with a thick, woody, elongate taproot. Stems are 1 to several and branched. Leaves are alternate, stalked, gland-dotted, palmately compound, with 3 or usually 5 elliptic to egg-shaped, entire, 1–2 ½ in.–long and ¼–1 in.–wide leaflets; upper leaf surface is green and mostly smooth, the lower surface is appressed-hairy. Inflorescences are dense, glandular, cylindrical spikes 1½–3½ in. long on long stalks arising from the bases of leaves. The calyx is 5-lobed and purplish, with the lower lobe about twice as long as the upper lobes; the 5 petals are blue to purple; stamens are 10, with 9 joined by their filaments and 1 free. Fruits are papery, ¼ in.–long, beaked legumes surrounded by the bladdery calyx; each contains a single smooth brownish seed.

Blooming Period
May–June.

Habitat
Mixed and shortgrass prairies and often on dry rocky slopes and around outcrops; C ½.

Psoralea esculenta Pursh

Breadroot scurf-pea,
Prairie turnip

Fabaceae
Bean Family

Description

Breadroot scurf-pea is a low, erect, spreading-hairy, perennial herb ¼–1 ft. tall, with a woody top-shaped taproot. Stems are 1 or few and mostly unbranched. Leaves are alternate, short-stalked to long-stalked, palmately compound, with 5 elliptic entire leaflets 1–2 in. long and about ½ in. wide, smooth or nearly so above, and appressed-hairy beneath. Inflorescences are dense cylindrical spikes 2–3 in. long on long stalks arising from the bases of leaves. The calyx is 5-lobed, with the lower lobe slightly longer than the upper ones; petals are 5, pale blue to blue, fading brown or yellowish, and up to ¾ in. long; stamens are 10, with 9 joined by their filaments and 1 free. Fruits are egg-shaped, beaked, smooth to glandular legumes containing a single brownish seed.

Blooming Period

May–July.

Habitat

Tallgrass, mixed, and shortgrass prairies, open woods, and roadsides; NE ½ and infrequent in SW.

The roots of this species once served as an important food source for the Plains Indians. Little breadroot scurf-pea (*P. hypogaea* Nutt.) is similar to breadroot scurf-pea but is stemless and has appressed hairs. It has been observed in widely scattered sites in the southwestern half of our region.

Psoralea tenuiflora Pursh

Wild alfalfa,
Scurfy pea

Fabaceae
Bean Family

Fruits* are smooth, egg-shaped, gland-dotted legumes, each containing a single brown kidney-shaped seed.

Blooming Period
May–July, sometimes also in September.

Habitat
All prairie types, roadsides, and occasionally in disturbed sites; throughout region.

This species is not closely related to cultivated alfalfa.

Two varieties occur in our region. Var. *tenuiflora* is found in the western two-thirds on mixed and shortgrass prairies. It is mostly appressed-hairy and densely glandular and has open inflorescences. Var. *floribunda* (Nutt.) Rydb. occurs on tallgrass prairies in the eastern third of the region; it typically is spreading-hairy and sparsely glandular and has dense spikes.

Description
Wild alfalfa is an erect, appressed-hairy, gland-dotted, perennial herb ½–4 ft. tall, with a deep woody taproot. Stems are 1 to many, multi-branched, and ridged. Leaves are alternate, stalked, and palmately compound, with leaflets that are lance-shaped to elliptic, entire, ½–2 in.–long, and less than ½ in.–wide; lower leaves have 5 leaflets, upper leaves have 3–4. Inflorescences are open to dense racemes at the ends of long stalks arising singly or in clusters from the bases of upper leaves. The calyx is 5-lobed, with the lower lobe slightly longer than the upper 4 and gland-dotted; petals are light blue to bluish purple and about ¼ in. long; stamens are 10, with 9 joined by their filaments and 1 free.

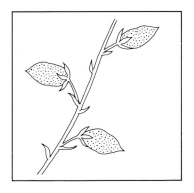

Psoralea argophylla Pursh

Silver-leaf scurf-pea

Fabaceae
Bean Family

several and branched above. Leaves are alternate, stalked, gland-dotted, and palmately compound, with elliptic to egg-shaped leaflets ½–1½ in. long and about ½ in. wide; lower leaves have 4–5 leaflets, upper ones have 3. Inflorescences are spikes on 1–3 in.–long stalks arising from the bases of upper leaves; they consist of 2–8 distinct few-flowered clusters each. The calyx is 5-lobed and silky, with the lower lobe longer than the upper 4; the 5 petals are purplish to bluish purple, fading brown or yellow, and up to ¼ in. long; stamens are 10, with 9 joined by their filaments and 1 free. Fruits are short, egg-shaped, beaked legumes, each containing a single brown kidney-shaped seed.

Blooming Period
June–September.

Description
Silver-leaf scurf-pea is an erect, silvery, silky, perennial herb ½–3 ft. tall, with a spreading woody root. Stems are 1 to

Habitat
All prairie types and open woodlands; primarily in N ½.

Dalea purpurea Vent.

Purple prairie-clover

Fabaceae
Bean Family

Description
Purple prairie-clover is a smooth to hairy perennial herb, with a thick woody root. Stems are ribbed, spreading to erect, and ½–3 ft. tall. Leaves are alternate, short-stalked, ½–2 in. long, ½–1 in. wide, and odd-pinnately compound, with 3–7 linear leaflets. Inflorescences are usually compact, densely flowered, cylindrical spikes produced at the ends of stems. Flowers are small; the calyx is 5-lobed and densely hairy; the petals are reddish purple to bluish purple; there are 5 stamens joined by their filaments. Fruits are small, smooth, egg-shaped legumes, each containing a single small brownish seed.

Blooming Period
May–August.

Habitat
Most prairie types, open woods, and roadsides and often in rocky soil; throughout region.

This species exhibits considerable variation. In sandy soil in the western half of our region, the plants are often shorter and smooth and bear smaller spikes than plants elsewhere. Purple prairie-clover is often found with white prairie-clover (*D. candida* Michx. ex. Willd.). Because *D. purpurea* is also a nutritious forb that is consumed by livestock, it decreases in heavily grazed prairies.

Dalea villosa (Nutt.) Spreng.

Silky prairie-clover

Fabaceae
Bean Family

Description
Silky prairie-clover is an ascending or spreading, densely spreading-hairy, perennial herb with a reddish-orange root. Stems are 1 to several, generally branched above, and ½–1½ ft. tall. Leaves are alternate, short-stalked, 1–2 in. long, ½–1 in. wide, and odd-pinnately compound, with 11–21 elliptic leaflets. Inflorescences are dense, elongate, cylindrical spikes sometimes drooping at the tip. Flowers are small; the calyx is 5-lobed and densely hairy; petals are lavender, pink, or whitish; there are 5 stamens joined by their filaments. Fruits are small hairy legumes each containing a single brown seed.

Blooming Period
June–August.

Habitat
Mixed, shortgrass, and sandsage prairies in sandy soil, especially on dunes along major rivers, and occasionally in open sandy woods; W ½.

Silky prairie-clover is common on dunes along the Arkansas, Cimarron, and Canadian rivers. Woolly dalea (*D. lanata* Spreng.) is common in similar habitats in the southern half of the region. It has prostrate stems, bluish-green leaves, and reddish-blue or violet flowers.

Evolvulvus nuttallianus R. & S.

Nuttall's evolvulus

Convolvulaceae
Morning Glory Family

Description
Nuttall's evolvulus is a low, erect or as-cending, somewhat woody, perennial herb 4–6 in. tall, covered with silky sil-very or rusty hairs, and arising from a woody rootstock. Stems are few to many. Leaves are alternate, simple, short-stalked or sessile, lance-shaped to egg-shaped, ¼–¾ in. long, and less than ¼ in. wide, with entire margins. Flowers are solitary and borne on short stalks at the bases of leaves. The calyx is 5-parted and spreading-silky; the corolla is wheel-shaped to shallowly funnel-shaped, up to ½ in. wide, pleated, and pale blue to lav-ender or whitish; stamens are 5. Fruits are small, smooth, spherical to egg-shaped capsules on drooping stalks, each containing 1–2 smooth brownish seeds.

Blooming Period
May–July.

Habitat
Rocky to sandy prairies; throughout most of region but scattered in NE ¼.

This species is named in honor of Thomas Nuttall, a nineteenth-century naturalist.

obelia spicata Lam.

Palespike lobelia

Campanulaceae
Bellflower Family

Description
Palespike lobelia is an erect, slender, sparingly hairy, perennial herb ½–3 ft.

tall, with fibrous roots. Stems are usually single and unbranched. Leaves are alternate, simple, stalked below to sessile above, elliptic to narrowly lance-shaped, ½–3 in. long, and ¼–1 in. wide, with entire to toothed margins. Inflorescences are terminal racemes up to 1 ft. long. Flowers are pale blue, 5-lobed, and up to ¼ in. long; corollas are 2-lipped, with the lower 3 lobes somewhat forward-projecting and the upper 2 erect; stamens are 5, with the filaments and blue anthers united and forming a tube around the style. Fruits are rounded capsules that contain numerous tiny brownish seeds.

Blooming Period
May–July.

Habitat
Tallgrass prairies and rarely in open woods; E ¼.

Monarda citriodora Cev. ex Lag.

Lemon mint,
Lemon beebalm

Lamiaceae
Mint Family

the ends of branches. Bracts below the flowers are densely short-hairy, bristle-tipped, and lavender or purplish; the calyx is 5-lobed, with bristle-like teeth; the corolla is white to pale lavender, up to 1 in. long, and 2-lipped, with the upper lip arched and the lower lip 3-lobed and often purple-spotted; stamens are 2 and hidden by the upper lip. Fruits are composed of 4 small, smooth, brownish nutlets, each containing a single seed.

Blooming Period
May–July.

Habitat
Sandy to rocky prairies, pastures, road sides, and occasionally in open woods; scattered throughout region but more common in S.

Description
Lemon mint is an erect, short-hairy, annual herb 1–3 ft. tall, with a slender tap-root. Stems are single, usually branched, and 4-angled. Leaves are opposite, simple, short-stalked, gland-dotted, lance-shaped to elliptic, ½–3 in. long, and ¼–¾ in. wide, with nearly entire to toothed margins. Inflorescences are 1–6 crowded leafy-bracted clusters of flowers in interrupted spikelike arrangements at

Spotted beebalm (*M. pectinata* Nutt.) is similar to lemon mint but has smooth flower bracts and shorter calyx teeth. It is widely scattered in the western half of our region and most common in the southwestern quarter. Dotted beebalm or horse mint (*M. punctata* L. subsp. *occidentalis* Epl.) has short triangular calyx teeth and is found most frequently in sandy sites, especially in the central third of the region.

Clematis pitcheri T. & G.

Pitcher's clematis

Ranunculaceae
Buttercup Family

Habitat
Rocky banks and slopes on tallgrass prairies and along streams and rivers; E ½.

This species honors Zina Pitcher, a U.S. Army physician who collected plants in the early 1830s.

Pitcher's clematis is most conspicuous when fruiting. Fremont's clematis (*C. fremontii* S. Wats.) has flowers and fruiting heads that are similar to Pitcher's clematis, but it is a low herb with simple leaves. In our region, Fremont's clematis is restricted to the Smoky Hills of north-central Kansas, where it is common.

Description
Pitcher's clematis is a climbing or scrambling, slightly woody, perennial vine. Stems are smooth to hairy and may grow over 15 ft. long. Leaves are opposite, stalked, and pinnately compound, with 3–11 widely spaced, entire or lobed, heart-shaped to elliptic leaflets; a tendril is often present at the tip of the leaves. Flowers are urnlike and produced on long stalks arising from the bases of leaves or leaflets; the 4 leathery, petallike sepals are hairy and brownish purple with recurved tips; true petals are absent. Fruits* are small disklike achenes borne in spherical clusters, with silky styles radiating outward.

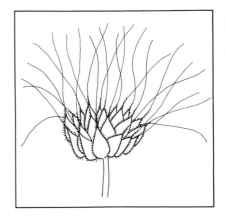

Blooming Period
May–August.

Verbena stricta Vent.

Hoary vervain

Verbenaceae
Vervain Family

Description

Hoary vervain is an erect, stout, densely hairy, perennial herb ½–4 ft. tall. Stems are 1 to several and sometimes branched. Leaves* are opposite, simple, mostly sessile, lance-shaped to elliptic, ¾–4 in. long, and ¼–2 in. wide, with toothed margins. Inflorescences are 1 to several slender, cylindrical, terminal spikes up to 1 ft. long. Flowers are 5-lobed; the calyx is less than ¼ in. long, densely hairy, with triangular lobes; the corolla is blue to bluish purple, shallowly funnel-shaped, and about ¼ in. wide, with spreading lobes; the 4 stamens are in 2 groups of different lengths. Fruits are composed of 4 slender, grayish brown, bumpy nutlets, each containing a single seed.

Blooming Period
May–September.

Habitat
Disturbed sites on all prairie types, pastures, roadsides, and waste areas; throughout region except in SW ¼.

Blue verbena (*V. hastata* L.) is a tall slender plant with narrowly lance-shaped leaves and dark blue flowers less than ¼ in. wide and borne in short crowded spikes. It inhabits moist sites throughout most of the northeastern two-thirds of our region. Narrow-leaved verbena (*V. simplex* Lehm.) is seldom over 1 ft. tall and has narrowly lance-shaped to linear leaves that are sessile and slender and solitary spikes with light blue to dark blue flowers. It is restricted to open rocky sites in the eastern quarter of the region.

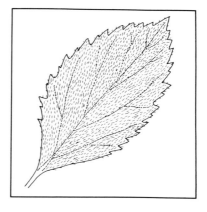

erbena bipinnatifida Nutt.

Dakota verbena

Verbenaceae
Vervain Family

Description
Dakota verbena is a low, spreading or ascending, somewhat hairy, perennial herb. Stems are several to many, multibranched from the base, ¼–2 ft. long, and often rooting at the nodes. Leaves* are opposite, stalked, egg-shaped to triangular in outline, ½–2 in. long, ½–2 in. wide, and 2–3 times pinnately divided, with linear or lance-shaped segments. Inflorescences are showy terminal spikes that are flattened at first but elongate in fruit. Flowers are 5-lobed; the calyx is over ¼ in. long, with uneven bristle-like lobes; the corolla is bluish purple to pink, tubular, ½–¾ in. long, with spreading lobes; stamens are 4, in 2

groups of different lengths. Fruits are composed of 4 slender pitted nutlets, each containing a single seed.

Blooming Period
May–October.

Habitat
All prairie types, pastures, and roadsides, usually on rocky slopes and outcrops; throughout region.

Prostrate verbena (*V. bracteata* Lag. & Rodr.) is a low creeping perennial with blue or bluish purple flowers less than ⅛ in. wide. It is particularly common on disturbed rocky ground and occurs throughout the region.

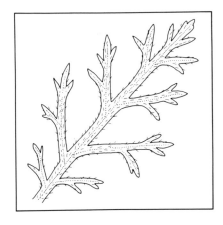

Solanum elaeagnifolium Cav

Silver-leaf nightshade,
White horse-nettle

Solanaceae
Nightshade Family

Description

Silver-leaf nightshade is an erect, silvery, perennial herb ¼–3 ft. tall and covered with tiny star-shaped hairs and a few short yellowish prickles. Stems often are branched and few to many from deep rhizomes. Leaves are alternate, simple, short-stalked, narrowly lance-shaped to egg-shaped, 1–6 in. long, and ½–1 in. wide, with entire, wavy, or toothed margins. Inflorescences are short racemelike clusters of 1–7 stalked flowers arising from the bases of leaves near the ends of branches. The calyx is 5-lobed; the corolla is 5-angled, flattened and shallowly funnel-shaped, light to dark blue or violet or rarely white, and ½–1¼ in. wide; the 5 stamens are yellow and prominent. Fruits* are spherical dark berries containing numerous brown seeds.

Blooming Period
May–October.

Habitat
Disturbed sites, including prairies, pastures, fields, roadsides, and waste areas; S ¾.

"Nightshade" refers to the medicinal use of *Solanum* species to induce sleep.

Commelina erecta L.

Erect dayflower

Commelinaceae
Spiderwort Family

Description
Erect dayflower is a weak-stemmed perennial herb that grows up to 2½ ft. tall. Stems are erect or spreading and watery. Leaves are alternate, narrowly lance-shaped to nearly elliptic, entire, smooth to sparingly hairy, 1–4 in. long, ½–1 in. wide, and parallel-veined, with a tubular sheath. Inflorescences are few-flowered clusters borne near the ends of stems and surrounded by leafy bracts. Flowers are 3-parted, with 2 large, blue, upper petals and 1 small, white, lower petal; there are 6 stamens, 3 of which are sterile. Fruits are small capsules, each containing 3 smooth brown seeds.

Blooming Period
May–October.

Habitat
Moist, rocky to sandy soil in prairies, along streams and riverbanks, and in pastures; throughout region.

Plants in the eastern half of our region tend to have broader leaves and are often found in rocky soil. In the western portion of the region, plants frequently grow in sandy soil.

Four species of dayflower occur in our region. Like erect dayflower, common dayflower (*C. communis* L.) has one white petal; however, its flower bracts are open at the base, whereas those of erect dayflower are fused. The other two species have three blue petals. As the common name indicates, the flowers remain open for only one day.

Cleome serrulata Pursh

Rocky Mountain bee plant

Capparaceae
Caper Family

than the petals. Fruits* are cylindrical capsules 1–2½ in. long, with tapering ends; each fruit contains few to many small mottled seeds.

Blooming Period
June–August.

Habitat
Open prairies, especially in sandy to rocky soil, open woodlands, and disturbed sites; NW ½ but less common in S.

The Capparaceae is closely related to the Brassicaceae (Mustard Family), and an examination of each family reveals many similarities. The Caper Family is best developed in the tropics and subtropics with most of its temperate members adapted to dry environments. The flower buds of the Mediterranean shrub *Capparis spinosa* L. are used as a condiment and seasoning known as capers.

Description
Rocky Mountain bee plant is an erect, smooth and somewhat waxy, annual herb 1–5 ft. tall. Stems are mostly single and branched above. Leaves are alternate, stalked, and palmately compound, with 3 narrowly lance-shaped entire leaflets 1–2 in. long and about ¼ in. wide. Inflorescences are elongate many-flowered racemes borne at the ends of branches. The 4 sepals are partly united; the petals are 4, bluish purple to pink, and up to ½ in. long; the 6 stamens have pink or purple filaments that are much longer

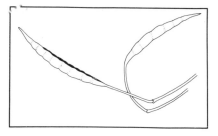

lifornia loosestrife

Lythraceae
Loosestrife Family

Blooming Period
June–September.

Habitat
Wet areas in tallgrass and mixed prairies, pastures, roadsides, and ditches and along streams, rivers, and ponds; SE ½.

Winged loosestrife (*L. alatum* Pursh) is highly similar to California loosestrife, and the two species are combined by some authors. California loosestrife tends to have narrower leaves that are waxy and firmer. Purple loosestrife (*L. salicaria* L.), a robust perennial with showy terminal spikes, is an aggressive wetland weed in many areas of the northeastern United States. It was introduced from Europe as a garden ornamental and is occasionally encountered in the region.

Description
California loosestrife is an erect, smooth, perennial herb 1–2½ ft. tall, arising from slender, fibrous-rooted rhizomes. Stems are 1 to several, branched, and slender. Leaves are alternate, simple, sessile, entire, gray-green, waxy, somewhat firm, narrowly lance-shaped to elliptic, ¼–1½ in. long, and less than ¼ in. wide. Flowers are single or paired and sessile and arise from the bases of leaves toward the ends of branches; the calyx is 6-lobed, the sepals alternating with 6 fleshy appendages; petals are dark lavender to purple and about ¼ in. long; there are usually 6 stamens. Fruits* are ribbed cylindrical capsules containing abundant small brownish seeds.

Ruellia humilis Nutt.

Fringeleaf ruellia

Acanthaceae
Acanthus Family

Description
Fringeleaf ruellia is an erect, smooth to spreading-hairy, perennial herb ¼–1½ ft. tall, with fibrous roots and sometimes thin rhizomes. Stems are single, branched, and somewhat angular. Leaves are opposite, simple, short-stalked to sessile, ascending, lance-shaped to broadly egg-shaped, 1–3 in. long, and ½–1½ in. wide, with entire and hairy margins. Inflorescences are few-flowered, sessile, and leafy-bracted and arise from the bases of middle and upper leaves.

Flowers are showy; the calyx is 5-lobed; the lavender to pale blue corolla is 5-lobed, trumpet-shaped, often with reddish lines within, 1½–3 in. long, ¾–1½ in. wide, and short-hairy; stamens are 4, in 2 groups of different lengths. Fruits are smooth, elongate, tan capsules about ½ in. long and contain numerous brownish seeds.

Blooming Period
June–September.

Habitat
Tallgrass prairies, open woodlands, roadsides, and pastures, especially in rocky soil; E ½.

The Acanthus Family includes some 2,500 species, most in the tropics. Many members are cultivated as ornamental houseplants, such as zebra plant (*Aphelandra squarrosa* Nees), shrimp plant (*Beloperone guttata* Brandegee), and crossandra (*Crossandra infundibuliformis* Nees).
   Limestone ruellia (*R. strepens* L.) is a taller, smooth, shade-loving plant found in woodlands and forests in the eastern third of the region.

n skeletonplant

Asteraceae
Sunflower Family

Description

Rush skeletonplant is an erect, wiry, smooth, perennial herb ½–2½ ft. tall, with yellow milky sap and a long, slender, vertical rhizome. Stems are gray-green and waxy, multi-branched from the base, and ribbed. Leaves are few and much-reduced; those on the lower stem are linear and less than 2 in. long; upper stem leaves are reduced to scales. Heads are cylindrical and solitary at the ends of branches. Bracts on the heads are 5–7 and linear; florets are 5 and raylike, lavender to pink, up to ½ in. long, and 5-toothed at the tip. Fruits are cylindrical, ribbed, ¼ in.–long achenes tipped with numerous slender bristles.

Blooming Period
June–September.

Habitat
Nearly all prairie types, especially in sandy to silty soil; W ¾.

The common name refers to the appearance of the branched, nearly leafless stem.

Monarda fistulosa L.

Wild bergamot

Lamiaceae
Mint Family

lobed and spreading; stamens are 2 and project beyond the upper lip. Fruits* are composed of 4 small dark nutlets, each containing a single seed.

Blooming Period
June–September.

Habitat
Rocky tallgrass and mixed prairies, pastures, roadsides, and occasionally open woods; E ½.

Oswego-tea (M. *didyma* L.) is a beautiful red-flowered species native to eastern North America and sometimes cultivated as an ornamental. Many species of *Monarda* have been used in the past for medicinal purposes. Dried leaves of wild bergamot make a tasty tea. The fragrance of dried flowers lasts for months, so they can be used in potpourri or sachets.

Description
Wild bergamot is an aromatic, erect, short-hairy, perennial herb 1–4 ft. tall, with slender branched rhizomes. Stems are usually clustered, branched above, brittle, and 4-angled. Leaves are opposite, simple, stalked, gland-dotted, lance-shaped to narrowly triangular, 1–4 in. long, and ½–2 in. wide, with nearly entire to coarsely toothed margins. Inflorescences are crowded, solitary terminal heads up to 3 in. wide and borne at the ends of branches. Bracts below the flowers are green to whitish; the calyx is 5-lobed, with long bristles; the corolla is pale to dark lavender or rarely white, up to 1½ in. long, strongly 2-lipped, with the upper lip slender, slightly arched, and hairy at the tip and the lower lip 3-

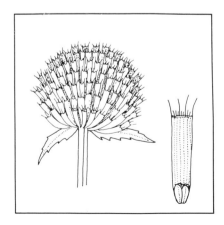

azurea Lam.

Lamiaceae

Mint Family

long, and ½–1 in. wide, with nearly entire to toothed margins. Inflorescences
are dense many-flowered clusters borne
in terminal, interrupted, spikelike arrangements. The calyx is short-hairy and
often tinged blue; the corolla is blue to
deep blue or rarely white, up to 1 in.
long, and 2-lipped, with the upper lip
short and densely hairy and the lower lip
broad and spreading; the 2 stamens are
hidden in the upper lip. Fruits are composed of 1–2 small, brown, resin-dotted
nutlets, each containing a single seed.

Blooming Period
June–October.

Habitat
Tallgrass and mixed prairies, roadsides,
and pastures, especially on rocky sites;
E ⅔.

Lance-leaved sage (*S. reflexa* Hornem.) is
a branched annual with ¼ in.–long pale-
blue to white flowers. It inhabits a wide
range of disturbed habitats throughout
the region. *S. officinalis* L. is the source of
the aromatic sage leaves used in cooking.

Description
Blue sage is an erect, short-hairy, perennial herb 1½–5 ft. tall, arising from a
thick rootstock. Stems are 1 to several,
sometimes branched, and 4-angled.
Leaves are opposite, simple, short-
stalked, lance-shaped to linear, 1–4 in.

Ipomoea purpurea (L.) Roth.

Common morning-glory

Convolvulaceae
Morning Glory Family

Description
Common morning-glory is a twining or trailing annual herb. Stems are slender, sometimes branched, loose-hairy, and up to 15 ft. long. Leaves* are alternate, simple, heart-shaped or occasionally 3-lobed, ½–4½ in. long, and ½–5 in. wide, with entire margins. Inflorescences are few-flowered clusters on short to long stalks arising from the bases of leaves. The calyx is 5-lobed, and the sepals are unequal; the corolla is funnel-shaped, up to 3 in. wide, slightly angular, pleated, bluish purple to red, with a white tube; stamens are 5. Fruits are smooth spherical capsules containing up to 6 angular, dark, short-hairy seeds.

Blooming Period
June–October.

Habitat
Disturbed sites, including roadsides, fields, pastures, and waste areas; NE ½.

Ivyleaf morning-glory (*I. hederacea* Jacq.) is also an introduced annual with a distribution similar to common morning-glory. It has 3-lobed or 5-lobed leaves and slightly smaller light-blue flowers.

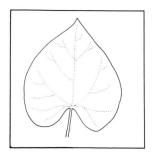

Strophostyles helvola (L.) Ell.

Trailing wildbean

Fabaceae
Bean Family

Description

Trailing wildbean is a trailing or climbing, spreading-hairy, annual herb, with a taproot. Stems are single, usually branched at the base and above, and ½–6 ft. long. Leaves are of 2 types: Lowermost leaves are opposite, simple, entire, and ¼–½ in. long; remaining leaves are alternate, stalked, pinnately compound, with 3 egg-shaped to broadly lance-shaped, ¾–3 in.–long, ¾–2 in.–wide, entire or 3-lobed leaflets. Inflorescences are few-flowered racemes on stalks up to 6 in. long arising from the bases of leaves. Flowers are 5-parted and about ½ in. long; petals are purple to rose, the upper one prominent; stamens are 10, 9 joined by their filaments and 1 free. Fruits* are slender, cylindrical, sparsely appressed-hairy, 1–4 in.–long legumes containing few brownish woolly seeds.*

Blooming Period
June–October.

Habitat
Moist prairies, floodplains, fields, pastures, roadsides, thickets, and open rocky woods; E ½.

Slick-seed wildbean [*S. leiosperma* (T. & G.) Piper] is similar to trailing wildbean but has flowers about ¼ in. long, smooth seeds, and narrower leaflets. It is common in a wide range of habitats throughout the region but is scattered in the western third.

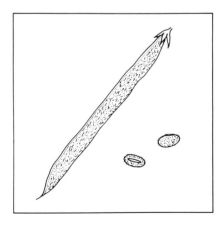

Proboscidea louisianica (P. Mill.) Thell.

Devil's claw,
Unicorn plant

Pedaliaceae
Unicorn-plant Family

Description
Devil's claw is an erect, sticky, glandular-hairy, fetid, annual herb ½–3 ft. tall, with a stout taproot. Stems are single, spreading-branched from the base, and thick. Leaves are opposite, occasionally alternate above, simple, long-stalked, heart-shaped to kidney-shaped, 2–9 in. long, and 2–10 in. wide, with entire to wavy margins. Inflorescences are terminal racemes 1½–12 in. long, with 4–30 flowers, and held above the leaves. Flowers are showy; the calyx is pinkish and 5-lobed, with the upper lobes longer than the lower ones; the corolla is funnel-shaped, up to 2 in. long, pale lavender to pink or white, the throat lined with dark yellow stripes and reddish spots, 2-lipped, the lower 3 lobes spreading and

the upper 2 erect; stamens are 5, with 1 or rarely 2–3 sterile. Fruits* are stout woody capsules up to 4 in. long, with 2 sharp curved claws at the tip, and contain many rough slightly flattened seeds.

Blooming Period
June–October.

Habitat
Disturbed sites, including fields, pastures, roadsides, and waste areas, often in sandy soil; throughout region but infrequent in E ⅓.

Dense stands are often seen in cultivated fields and pastures in the western third of our region. The distinctive clawed fruits are adapted nicely for dispersal via the legs and fur of passing animals.

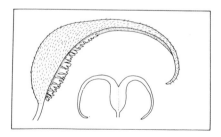

Machaeranthera tanacetifolia (H.B.K.) Nees

Tansy aster,
Tahoka daisy

Asteraceae
Sunflower Family

Description
Tansy aster is a spreading and somewhat busy, glandular-hairy, annual herb ¼—1½ ft. tall, arising from a taproot. Stems are single and usually multi-branched from the base. Leaves are alternate, short-stalked to sessile, crowded, 1–3 in. long, up to 1 in. wide, and 1–2 times pinnately compound, with the smallest segments lance-shaped to linear. Heads are solitary at the ends of upper branches. Bracts on the heads are papery at the base but green and spreading at the tip; ray florets are numerous, blue to purplish, and up to ¾ in. long; disk florets are abundant and small. Fruits are small appressed-hairy achenes tipped with stiff slender bristles.

Blooming Period
July–September.

Habitat
Mixed, shortgrass, and sandsage prairies, roadsides, and disturbed sites, often in sandy soil; W ½.

Machaeranthera is closely related to *Aster,* and species have been placed in the latter genus by various authors. Tansy aster is an attractive plant and is occasionally cultivated as an ornamental.

Liatris pycnostachya Michx.

Thickspike gayfeather

Asteraceae
Sunflower Family

Description
Thickspike gayfeather is a stiff, erect, perennial herb 2–5 ft tall, arising from a woody corm. Stems are 1 to several, unbranched, and hairy above. Leaves are al ternate, simple, mostly sessile, numerous, gradually reduced up the stem, entire, linear, ½–8 in. long, and less than ½ in. wide. Inflorescences are elongate wandlike spikes up to 2½ ft. long, with numerous cylindrical heads less than ½ in. long. Bracts on the heads are gland-dotted and often purplish, with the tips usually spreading; ray florets are absent; disk florets are 5–10, lavender to reddish purple, and smooth inside. Fruits are short, hairy, ribbed, brownish achenes tipped with finely barbed bristles.

Blooming Period
July–September.

Habitat
Tallgrass prairies, especially in moist draws and low areas; E ½

Cultivated varieties of *Liatris* are available and are grown for the cut-flower market. Flowering spikes can be air-dried for use in winter arrangements.

tris punctata Hook.

Dotted gayfeather

Asteraceae
Sunflower Family

Description
Dotted gayfeather is an erect, smooth, gland-dotted,* perennial herb ½–2½ ft. tall, arising from a woody taproot. Stems are usually clustered and unbranched. Leaves* are alternate, simple, sessile, numerous, gradually reduced up the stem, linear, ½–6 in. long, and less than ¼ in. wide, with entire margins. Inflorescences are dense wandlike spikes up to 1 ft. long, with numerous cylindrical ½ in.– long heads. Bracts on the heads are narrow and tapering; ray florets are absent; disk florets are 4–8, lavender to reddish purple, and resinous-hairy inside. Fruits are short, dark brown, ribbed achenes tipped with numerous feathery bristles.

Blooming Period
July–October.

Habitat
Dry rocky prairies of all types; throughout region.

Gayfeather (*L. mucronata* DC.) is distinguished from dotted gayfeather only with difficulty. It has a rounded corm and lacks hairs along the leaf margins. Gayfeather is found in the eastern third of our region and infrequently westward. Blazing star [*L. squarrosa* (L.) Michx.] is a smooth to hairy plant with 10–60 florets per head and feathery bristles at the tips of the achenes. It occurs on prairies and in open woods primarily in the eastern half of the region.

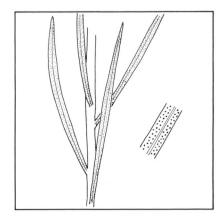

Liatris aspera Michx.

Button blazing star

Asteraceae
Sunflower Family

Description
Button blazing star is an erect, smooth to short-hairy, perennial herb 1½–4 ft. tall, arising from a woody corm. Stems are 1 to several and unbranched. Leaves are alternate, simple, short-stalked below but sessile above, gradually reduced up the stem, entire, narrowly lance-shaped to linear, 1½–8 in. long, and ¼–1½ in. wide. Inflorescences are elongate, wand-like spikes up to 1½ ft. long, with few to many bell-shaped heads. Bracts on the heads are rounded and often purplish; ray florets are absent; disk florets are 16–40, lavender to pale purple, and resinous-hairy inside. Fruits are short, hairy, ribbed, brown to blackish brown achenes tipped with numerous finely barbed bristles.

Blooming Period
August–October.

Habitat
Dry, rocky, tallgrass prairies and open woods; E ⅓.

ernonia baldwinii Torr.

Inland ironweed

Asteraceae
Sunflower Family

Description
Inland ironweed is an erect, sparingly hairy to woolly, perennial herb 2½–5 ft. tall. Stems are 1 to several and mostly unbranched and arise from rhizomes with fibrous roots. Leaves are alternate, simple, short-stalked, numerous, lance-shaped to narrowly egg-shaped, 1½–7 in. long, and 1–2½ in. wide, with toothed margins. Inflorescences are open to dense terminal clusters of bell-shaped heads about ¼ in. wide. Bracts on the heads are greenish brown to purple and gland-dotted, with spreading or recurved tips; ray florets are absent; disk florets are 17–34 and reddish purple to purple. Fruits are short, ribbed, smooth to hairy achenes tipped with numerous light brown to purplish bristles.

Blooming Period
July–October.

Habitat
Nearly all prairie types, pastures, road-sides, open woods, and disturbed sites; E ¾.

Western ironweed (*V. fasciculata* Michx.) is similar to inland ironweed but is mostly smooth and has conspicuous pits on the lower surface of the leaves and rounded bracts on the heads. It occurs in the northeastern quarter of our region. Plains ironweed [*V. marginata* (Torr.) Raf.] is found on shortgrass prairies in the southwestern quarter. It looks much like western ironweed but has more-pointed bracts.

Cirsium altissimum (L.) Spreng.

Tall thistle,
Roadside thistle

Asteraceae
Sunflower Family

Description
Tall thistle is an erect, hairy, biennial herb 3–8 ft. tall, with a fleshy taproot. Stems are branched above. Leaves are alternate, simple, green, mostly smooth above but white-woolly beneath, lance-shaped to elliptic, shallowly pinnately lobed, 4–12 in. long, 1½–4 in. wide, progressively smaller up the stem, and with short spines along the irregularly toothed margins. Heads are single, bell-shaped to urn-shaped, and produced at the ends of branches. Bracts on the heads each bear a spreading yellow spine at the tip; ray florets are absent; disk florets are light to dark purple or occasionally white. Fruits are small brownish achenes topped with white or gray feathery bristles.

Blooming Period
August–October.

Habitat
Tallgrass and mixed prairies, pastures, roadsides, and disturbed sites; E ½.

Leavenworth eryngo

Apiaceae
Parsley Family

Description

Leavenworth eryngo is an erect, glabrous, spiny annual 1½–3 ft. tall. Stems are waxy and multi-branched. Leaves are alternate, simple, sessile or short-stalked, spatula-shaped to egg-shaped, up to 3 in. long, and 1 in. wide and bear short stiff spines along the wavy margins; upper leaves are deeply palmately lobed. Inflorescences are dense, purplish, headlike clusters borne at the ends of branches, with spiny, purple, pinnately lobed bracts 1–2 in. long surrounding the bases. The small whitish flowers are 5-parted. Fruits are dry and oblong, with 2 segments covered with tiny white scales.

Blooming Period

July–October.

Habitat

Tallgrass prairies, open woodlands, pastures, and roadsides, usually in rocky limestone soil; E ⅓.

This striking thistle-like plant is often found with willow-leaved sunflower (*Helianthus salicifolius* A. Dietr.). The dried inflorescences hold their color well. The species name honors Melines Conklin Leavenworth, a U.S. Army surgeon who collected plants in the South and West during the 1830s.

Rattlesnake master or button snakeroot (*E. yuccifolium* Michx.) is a stout, yuccalike relative found on tallgrass prairies in the eastern third of our region. It has dense spherical heads and linear leaves.

Aster oblongifolius Nutt.

Aromatic aster

Asteraceae
Sunflower Family

Description
Aromatic aster is a sparsely hairy perennial herb ½–2 ft. tall, typically with glands on the stems and leaves and especially above. Stems are erect and multibranched, arising from a rhizome or woody rootstock. Leaves are alternate, simple, mostly oblong, ½–3 in. long, up to ½ in. wide, entire, and weakly clasping; the lower leaves are usually absent on flowering plants. Inflorescences are panicle-like with few to many heads borne near the ends of branches. Bracts on the head are glandular; ray florets are 25–30, bluish to bluish purple, and less than ½ in. long; disk florets are yellow. Fruits are small, somewhat flattened achenes tipped with abundant slender yellowish-white bristles.

Blooming Period
September–October.

Habitat
Dry, open, rocky to sandy, tallgrass and mixed prairies; E ⅔.

Silky aster (*A. sericeus* Vent.) is often found with aromatic aster on prairies in the northeastern quarter of our region, especially in the Flint Hills. It lacks glands on the leaves and stems but has silky hairs on the leaves.

, puberulenta Pringle

Gentianaceae

Gentian Family

Description
Downy gentian is an erect, minutely hairy, perennial herb ½–1½ ft. tall. Stems are 1 to several, mostly un-branched, and stout. Leaves are opposite, simple, sessile, shiny green above, lance-shaped to egg-shaped, ½–2 in. long, and ¼–1 in. wide, with entire margins. Inflorescences are dense clusters of 3–10 showy flowers at the ends of stems. The calyx is 5-lobed; the corolla is 5-lobed, funnel-shaped to bell-shaped, pleated, deep blue to bluish purple, 1–1½ in. long and about as wide, with spreading lobes; stamens are 5. Fruits are smooth elongate capsules, often surrounded by the persistent calyx and corolla, and contain small angular seeds.

Blooming Period
September–October.

Habitat
Tallgrass prairies; E ¼.

The dazzling blue flowers of this species are always welcome sights on prairies. It is among the last of our Great Plains wildflowers to bloom and often persists until the first hard frosts of fall.

Yellow or Orange

....lis micrantha (Engelm.) A. Gray

....der fumewort

Fumariaceae
Fumewort Family

upward-curved capsules up to 1 in. long and contain many small, shiny, black seeds.

Blooming Period
March–May.

Habitat
Tallgrass prairies, open woods, and disturbed sites, including roadsides, fields, and waste areas; E ½ but less common in W.

Five species of fumewort occur in our region, with slender fumewort among the most common and widely distributed. Golden fumewort (*C. aurea* Willd.) is found in the southern half of the region and has larger seeds than slender fumewort. Pale fumewort [*C. flavula* (Raf.) DC.] has a shorter spur than slender fumewort and occurs along floodplains in the eastern quarter of the region.

Description
Slender fumewort is an erect or spreading, smooth, often waxy, winter annual 4–12 in. tall, arising from a taproot. Stems are usually several and branched from the base. Leaves are alternate, stalked below to sessile above, egg-shaped in outline, 2–3½ in. long, and pinnately compound, with the smallest segments mostly elliptic. Inflorescences are 6–20 flowered racemes produced at the ends of branches. Flowers are irregular with 4 pale yellow petals, one of which bears a short spur; the 6 stamens are in 2 groups of 3. Fruits* are erect or

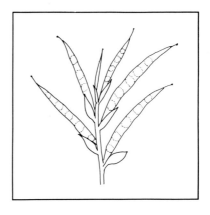

Lomatium foeniculaceum (Nutt.) Coult. & Ros.

Wild parsley

Apiaceae
Parsley Family

Habitat
Dry, rocky, tallgrass and mixed prairies and open woods; E ½.

A second species of wild parsley, *L. orientale* Coult. & Rose, has whitish flowers and is found predominantly in the northeastern quarter of our region. It is readily grazed by cattle and consequently occurs mostly in ungrazed sites, such as cemeteries with native vegetation.

Garden parsley is a native of Europe and in a different genus of the Apiaceae.

Description
Wild parsley is a low, stemless, smooth to hairy, perennial herb ¼–1½ ft. tall, with a slender to thick taproot. Leaves are alternate, stalked, broadly egg-shaped in outline, ½–8 in. long, and 2–3 times pinnately compound, with the smallest divisions mostly linear. Inflorescences are flat or slightly rounded compound umbels up to 4 in. wide and borne on naked stalks typically longer than the leaves. Flowers* are small, yellow to yellowish green, and 5-parted. Fruits* are dry and egg-shaped, with 2 smooth to hairy winged segments.

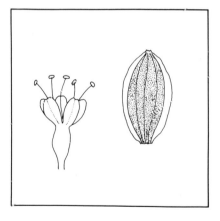

Blooming Period
March–May.

bracteata Muhl. ex Ell. var. *glabrescens*
(...y) Isley

...-bracted wild indigo

Fabaceae
Bean Family

white indigo [*B. lactea* (Raf.) Thieret] occurs in the eastern quarter of the region but is taller than long-bracted wild indigo, with waxy leaves and stems and white flowers on a tall, erect stalk. It grows on prairies and along the margins of woods and generally flowers later than long-bracted wild indigo and wild blue indigo.

Description
Long-bracted wild indigo is a robust perennial herb ¾–2½ ft. tall. Stems are multi-branched above. Leaves are alternate and sessile, usually with 3 lance-shaped or elliptic leaflets 1–4 in. long and ¼–1 in. wide. Inflorescences are drooping or spreading, showy, dense racemes. The large flowers are pale to dark yellow with a prominent upper petal; the 10 stamens are separate. Fruits* are inflated, hairy, beaked legumes 1–2 in. long and contain brownish seeds.

Blooming Period
April–June.

Habitat
Rocky tallgrass prairies; E ⅓.

The dead flowering stems of this and other wild indigos are frequently found on prairies in the fall and winter. Wild

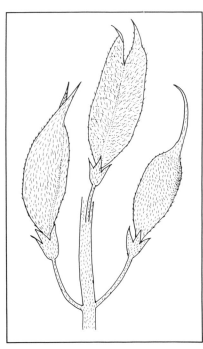

Erysimum asperum (Nutt.) DC.

Western wallflower

Brassicaceae
Mustard Family

Description
Western wallflower is an erect annual
¾–3 ft. tall and covered with a dense
layer of appressed branched hairs. Stems
are single, usually branched above, and
ridged. Leaves are alternate, simple, sessile, numerous, linear to lance-shaped,
½-4 in. long, mostly less than ½ in.
wide, with entire to toothed margins. Inflorescences are showy terminal racemes.
Flowers are 4-parted; the petals are
bright yellow to yellow-orange and up to
¾ in. long; there are 6 stamens, 4 of
them long and 2 short. Fruits* are
spreading, slender, 4-angled pods 3–5 in.
long that contain numerous small seeds.

Blooming Period
April–June.

Habitat
Dry, open, sandy to silty, shortgrass,
mixed, and sandsage prairies, pastures,

and roadsides; W ⅔ but infrequent in
Red Hills of Kansas and Oklahoma.

This attractive mustard forms highly visible patches, especially in short vegetation. The long, spreading fruits also
make it easy to find after flowering is
completed.
  Bushy wallflower (*E. repandum* L.) is a
smaller-flowered relative found throughout most of the region. It is a weed introduced from Europe and is found frequently in disturbed sites, fields,
pastures, and waste areas.

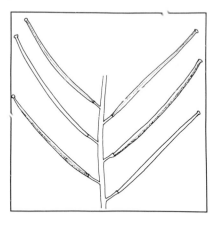

...lla ovalifolia Rydb.

...leaf bladderpod

Brassicaceae
Mustard Family

Description
Oval-leaf bladderpod is a low, sometimes tufted, ascending, perennial herb 3–8 in. tall and covered with a dense silvery coat of star-shaped hairs. Stems are few to many and arise from a branched, woody rootstock. Leaves are alternate, simple, stalked below and sessile above, entire, elliptic to spatula-shaped or nearly linear above, ¼–2½ in. long, and ¼–¾ in. wide. Inflorescences are compact terminal racemes of bright yellow flowers. The calyx and corolla are 4-parted; petals are up to ½ in. long; there are 6 stamens, 4 long and 2 short. Fruits* are dry, 2-parted, spherical capsules that contain few flattened brownish seeds.

Blooming Period
April–June.

Habitat
Mixed and shortgrass prairies, especially on dry, rocky, limestone or gypsum outcrops; W ½.

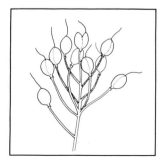

Lithospermum incisum Lehm.

Fringed puccoon

Boraginaceae
Borage Family

Description

Fringed puccoon is an erect, hairy, perennial herb ¼–1½ ft. tall, arising from a stout woody root. Stems are 1 to several and usually branched above. Leaves are alternate, simple, sessile, entire, linear to narrowly lance-shaped, ½–2 in. long, and mostly less than ¼ in. wide. Inflorescences are terminal slightly coiled clusters. Flowers are sessile; the calyx is 5-lobed; the corolla is 5-lobed, trumpet-shaped, and pale yellow to yellow, with fringed lobes; stamens are 5. Fruits are composed of 4 small, smooth or pitted, shiny, white, egg-shaped nutlets, each containing a single seed.

Blooming Period

April–June.

Habitat

All prairie types and in open dry woods; throughout region.

Fringed puccoon produces two kinds of flowers. Large showy ones seen in the early spring are cross-pollinated. Smaller inconspicuous flowers often lacking a corolla are produced in the late spring and summer and are self-pollinated. "Puccoon" is an Indian name for this genus.

Lithospermum carolinense (Walt.) MacM.

Puccoon,   Boraginaceae
Carolina puccoon   Borage Family

Description
Puccoon is an erect, rough-hairy, perennial herb ½–1½ ft. tall, with a thick reddish taproot. Stems are 1 to several and
sometimes branched. Leaves are alternate, simple, sessile, often crowded,
linear to lance-shaped, 1–2½ in. long,
and mostly less than ½ in. wide, with
entire margins. Inflorescences are terminal, slightly coiled clusters. Flowers are
showy and sessile; the calyx is 5-lobed;
the bright orange to yellow orange corolla is 5-lobed and funnel-shaped to
trumpet-shaped; there are 5 stamens.
Fruits are composed of 4 small, smooth,
shiny, white, egg-shaped nutlets, each
containing a single seed.

Blooming Period
May–June.

Habitat
Tallgrass prairies, sand prairies, and
open woods, especially in sandy soil;
scattered in E ½.

Hoary puccoon [*L. canescens* (Michx.)
Lehm.] is similar to puccoon but is soft-
hairy and has a shorter calyx. It is found
in the eastern quarter of our region and
seldom occurs in sandy soils. Corn
gromwell (*L. arvense* L.) is an introduced
annual with small whitish flowers. It occurs in disturbed sites in the eastern half
of the region.

Microseris cuspidata (Pursh) Sch.-Bip.

False dandelion

Asteraceae
Sunflower Family

Blooming Period
April–June.

Habitat
Dry sandy to rocky prairies of all types;
N ⅔.

Although occasionally confused with
common dandelion (*Taraxacum officinale*
Weber), this species can be recognized
by its entire leaves and beakless achenes.
False dandelion is native to our region.

Description
False dandelion is a stemless, smooth to
woolly, perennial herb ¼–1 ft. tall, with
milky sap and a taproot. Leaves are clustered in a basal rosette, linear to lance-
shaped, entire, 4–12 in. long, and up to
¾ in. wide, with woolly and wavy margins and a whitish midrib. Heads are solitary and bell-shaped and borne on short
to long, naked, flowering stalks. Bracts
on the heads are up to 1 in. long, and
linear to narrowly lance-shaped; florets
are numerous, yellow, and all raylike.
Fruits* are cylindrical, prominently
nerved, ¼ in.–long achenes tipped with
numerous slender bristles.

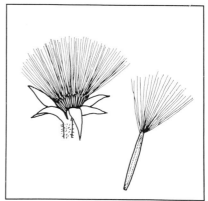

cio plattensis Nutt.

Prairie ragwort,
Prairie groundsel

Asteraceae
Sunflower Family

Description
Prairie ragwort is an erect, unevenly woolly, biennial or short-lived perennial herb ¼–2½ ft. tall, with a short woody rootstock. Stems are 1 or rarely several and mostly unbranched. Leaves are alternate, stalked below to sessile above, and gradually reduced up the stem; basal leaves are elliptic to egg-shaped, ½–4 in. long, and ¼–2 in. wide, with toothed margins; stem leaves are nearly entire to deeply pinnately lobed. Heads are few to many, up to 1 in. wide, bell-shaped, and on long slender stalks in terminal flat-topped clusters. Ray florets usually are 8, golden-yellow, and less than ½ in. long; disk florets are similar in color and nu-

merous. Fruits are smooth to short-hairy angular achenes tipped with abundant slender white bristles.

Blooming Period
April–June.

Habitat
Nearly all prairie types, particularly in rocky soil; throughout region except in SW ¼.

Plains ragwort (*S. tridenticulatus* Rydb.) is smooth or very sparingly hairy and has a taproot. It is encountered on the high plains in the western third of our region.

Sphaeralcea coccinea (Pursh) Rydb.

Scarlet globe mallow,
Red false mallow

Malvaceae
Mallow Family

Blooming Period
April–August.

Habitat
Dry, sandy to gravelly, mixed and short-grass prairies; W ⅔.

Several species of *Sphaeralcea* are widespread and conspicuous elements of the flora of the western United States. Narrowleaf globe mallow [*S. angustifolia* (Cav.) D. Don] enters our region in the southwestern quarter. It has lance-shaped leaves, flowers in open, elongate, panicle-like arrangements, and grows to 6 ft. tall.

Description
Scarlet globe mallow is a low, erect, gray-green, perennial herb ¼–1 ft. tall, covered with tiny star-shaped hairs and with a creeping woody rootstock. Stems are single or clustered and sometimes branched. Leaves are alternate, stalked, ½–2½ in. long, ½–1½ in. wide, and divided, with 3–5 wedge-shaped to egg-shaped, entire or toothed lobes. Inflorescences are terminal racemes 1–5 in. long or solitary flowers arising from the bases of leaves. The calyx is 5-lobed; the 5 petals are reddish orange to brick red or pink and ¼–¾ in. long; the numerous yellow stamens are united into a column. Fruits* are rings of 10 wrinkled, somewhat hairy, kidney-shaped segments containing few brown seeds.

Linum rigidum Pursh

Stiff flax

Linaceae
Flax Family

Description

Stiff flax is an erect, compact to spreading, smooth or sparingly hairy, annual herb 2–20 in. tall, with a slender taproot. Stems are single but typically multi-branched above. Leaves are alternate, simple, sessile, sometimes with small glands at the base, linear to narrowly lance-shaped, ½–1 in. long, and less than ⅛ in. wide, with entire to sparingly toothed margins; lower stem leaves are often absent on flowering plants. Flowers are borne in open to compact, somewhat flat, panicle-like clusters, mostly toward the ends of branches; sepals are 5 and glandular-toothed; the 5 petals are yellow or with an orange to brick-red base and up to ½ in. long; stamens are 5, with yellow anthers. Fruits* are yellowish, smooth, 5-segmented, egg-shaped capsules containing few small brownish seeds.

Blooming Period
April–September.

Habitat
Mixed, shortgrass, and sand prairies and in sandy to gravelly soil; W ⅔.

This highly variable species consists of three fairly distinct varieties differing in style length, fruit texture and shape, and presence or absence of glands at the bases of leaves. The plant shown here is var. *berlandieri* (Hook.) T. & G., or Berlandier's flax. Another species of *Linum* is the source of flax, a fiber used to weave linen.

Taraxacum officinale Weber

Common dandelion

Asteraceae
Sunflower Family

Description
Common dandelion is a stemless perennial herb, with milky sap and a deep taproot. Leaves are clustered in a low basal rosette, smooth to sparingly hairy, spatula-shaped in outline, toothed to deeply pinnately lobed, 2½–12 in. long, and ½–2 in. wide. Inflorescences are solitary 1–2 in.–wide heads at the ends of naked, hollow, flowering stalks 2–16 in. long. The numerous yellow florets are all raylike. Fruiting heads are spherical with recurved bracts; fruits* are tanned, short-spiny yellowish or tan achenes with an umbrella like cluster of slender white bristles at the top.

Blooming Period
April–October but capable of flowering year-round if conditions permit.

Habitat
Disturbed sites, especially in lawns, gardens, pastures, fields, and waste places; throughout region.

Common dandelion is a frequent lawn weed throughout much of North America. It was introduced from Europe and has become a naturalized part of the flora. Roots, leaves, and flower heads are edible. Red-seeded dandelion [*T. laevigatum* (Willd.) DC.] also occurs throughout much of the region and has reddish to brownish red achenes. The name "dandelion" apparently comes from the French *dent de lion* (lion's tooth), perhaps referring to the toothed leaves.

...hopappus grandiflorus (Nutt.) Nutt.

...uber false dandelion

Asteraceae
Sunflower Family

Description
Tuber false dandelion is a stemless, smooth to loosely hairy, perennial herb ½–1 ft. tall, with milky sap and a long cylindrical taproot bearing a rounded tuber 2–4 in. below the soil surface.

Leaves are clustered in a basal rosette, coarsely toothed to pinnately divided with toothed lobes, 1–9 in. long, and 1–2 in. wide. Heads are solitary, cylindrical to bell-shaped, and borne on flowering stalks up to 1 ft. long. Bracts on the heads are up to ¾ in. long and linear; florets are numerous, yellow, and all ray-like. Fruits are cylindrical, beaked, 5-ribbed achenes with numerous slender tan bristles.

Blooming Period
May–June.

Habitat
Tallgrass, mixed, and sand prairies, often in disturbed sites; C ⅓.

Pyrrhopappus carolinianus (Walt.) DC., known as false dandelion [see also *Microseris cuspidata* (Pursh) Sch.-Bip.], is an annual or biennial with leafy stems. It is found on disturbed prairies, along roadsides, and in pastures and waste areas in the eastern third of our region.

Polytaenia nuttallii DC.

Prairie parsley

Apiaceae
Parsley Family

wide, and gradually reduced up the stem. Inflorescences are flat or slightly rounded, loose, compound umbels 2–5 in. wide; the smaller umbels are crowded and on long spreading stalks. Flowers* are small, yellow or greenish yellow, and 5-parted. Fruits* are elliptic to nearly round and dry, with 2 ribbed segments ¼ in. long.

Blooming Period
May–June.

Habitat
Tallgrass prairies, especially in rocky limestone soil; E ⅓.

Description
Prairie parsley is an erect, stout, short-hairy, perennial herb 1–3 ft. tall, with a taproot. Stems are single and branched above. Leaves are alternate, with stalks up to 6 in. long, triangular in outline, 2–3 times pinnately compound, with egg-shaped to wedge-shaped and toothed leaflets that are 2½–7 in. long, 2½–6 in.

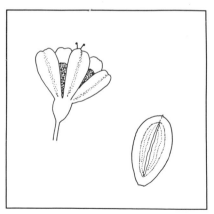

osia virginiana (L.) Pers.

oat's rue,
Catgut

Fabaceae
Bean Family

pale yellow to lemon yellow upper petal, with remaining petals pink to dark pink or rose; all 10 stamens are joined by their filaments. Fruits* are 1–2 in.–long, flattened, hairy legumes containing 3–8 dark mottled seeds.

Blooming Period
May–June.

Habitat
Tallgrass, mixed, and sand prairies, open woods, and roadsides and infrequently on shortgrass prairies; E ½ and scattered in SW ¼.

This plant used to be fed to goats to increase their milk production.

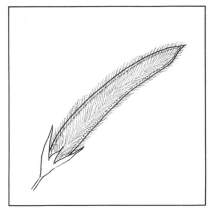

Description
Goat's rue is an erect, hairy, perennial herb ¾–2½ ft. tall, arising from a branched rootstock. Stems are few to many and sometimes branched. Leaves are alternate, short-stalked, 2–6 in. long, and odd-pinnately compound, with 7–31 elliptic to lance-shaped entire leaflets ¼–1¼ in. long. Inflorescences are showy, mostly terminal racemes 1–4 in. long. Flowers are 5-parted and up to ¾ in. long; the corolla has a prominent, erect,

Oenothera macrocarpa Nutt.

Evening primrose

Onagraceae
Evening Primrose Family

Description
Evening primrose is a low, occasionally tufted, smooth to hairy, perennial herb ¼–2 ft. tall. Stems are few to many, spreading to ascending, sometimes branched, and often reddish and arising from a thick woody root. Leaves are alternate, simple, stalked to sessile, narrowly lance-shaped to egg-shaped, 1–6 in. long, and ¼–1½ in. wide, with entire to shallowly toothed margins. Flowers are showy and solitary and arise from the bases of leaves; sepals are 4, reflexed, and often red-spotted; petals are 4, yellow, ¾–2½ in. long and nearly as wide, and at the end of a 2–5 in.–long floral tube; stamens are 8. Fruits* are prominently 4-winged capsules up to 4 in. long, each containing many small, angular, corky seeds.

Blooming Period
May–June.

Habitat
All prairie types, bluffs, and roadsides, especially on rocky limestone soils; E ¾.

Four semidistinct subspecies occur in the region. Missouri evening primrose (subsp. *macrocarpa*) is an appressed-hairy greenish plant with 1–2 in.–long petals that is found mostly in the northeastern quarter of our region. Hoary evening primrose [subsp. *incana* (A. Gray) W. L. Wagner] is similar to Missouri evening primrose but is silvery-hairy. It occurs in the southwestern quarter. Fremont's evening primrose [subsp. *fremontii* (S. Wats.) W. L. Wagner] has smaller ½–1 in.–long petals and is restricted to the north-central third of the region. Oklahoma evening primrose [subsp. *oklahomensis* (Nort.) W. L. Wagner] is a smooth phase found in the southeastern quarter.

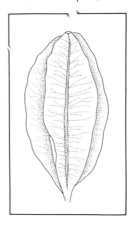

...ophus lavandulifolius (T. & G.) Raven

...vender leaf evening primrose   Onagraceae
Evening Primrose Family

crowded, linear to narrowly lance-shaped, ¼–2 in. long, and less than ¼ in. wide. Flowers are mostly solitary and up to 2½ in. long and arise from the bases of leaves near the ends of branches; the sepals are 4 and often with purple stripes along the margins; the 4 petals are 1½–2½ in. across and yellow, fade pinkish or purplish and form a slender tube at the base; there are 8 stamens. Fruits are 4-angled capsules ¼–1 in. long and contain numerous small, gray-hairy, angular seeds.

Blooming Period
May–August.

Habitat
Dry, gravelly to sandy, shortgrass and mixed prairies, often along rock outcrops; W ½.

Description
Lavender leaf evening primrose is a short, often tufted, herbaceous to slightly woody perennial, with a stout woody rootstock. Stems are usually branched, appressed gray-hairy, and ¼–1 ft. tall. Leaves are alternate, sessile, simple,

Hartweg's evening primrose [*C. hartwegii* (Benth.) Raven] is a closely related species found throughout the southwestern quarter of our region, often in mixed populations with lavender leaf evening primrose. It is distinguished from the latter by its smooth to slightly hairy stems.

Calylophus serrulatus (Nutt.) Raven

Plains yellow evening primrose

Onagraceae
Evening Primrose Family

Description
Plains yellow evening primrose is a multi-branched, herbaceous or shrubby perennial ½–2½ ft. tall, with a woody taproot. Stems are usually branched from the base, erect, and smooth to hairy. Leaves are alternate, sessile, simple, narrowly lance-shaped, ¼–4 in. long, and mostly less than ¼ in. wide, with entire to toothed margins. Flowers are showy, solitary, and up to 1 in. long and arise from the bases of upper leaves; the 4 sepals are green and reflexed and have a prominent ridge along the midrib; the 4 bright yellow petals form a short slender tube at the base and are roughly 1½ in. across; there are 8 stamens. Fruits* are 4-angled capsules ½–1 in. long and contain many small, brown, angular seeds.

Blooming Period
May–September.

Habitat
Nearly all prairie types, especially in rocky or gravelly soil; throughout region.

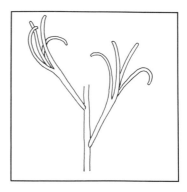

Coreopsis grandiflora Hogg ex Sweet

Bigflower coreopsis

Asteraceae
Sunflower Family

Description
Bigflower coreopsis is an erect or spreading, mostly glabrous, perennial herb 1–3 ft. tall. Stems are single or clustered and branched and arise from a short rhizome. Leaves are opposite, 1–4 in. long, and deeply pinnately divided, with 3–5 narrow linear segments. The 1–2 in.–wide heads are borne on long naked stalks arising from the ends of branches. Bracts on the heads are lance-shaped, with whitish margins; the 7–9 ray florets are yellow and up to 1 in. long and have 4 prominent lobes; disk florets are deep yellow and 5-lobed. Fruits are thin, flat, black achenes with wings and 2 small scales at the tip.

Blooming Period
May–July.

Habitat
Tallgrass prairies on rocky to sandy uplands and slopes, along roadsides, and occasionally in open woods; SE ⅓.

Beautiful flowering displays of bigflower coreopsis can be observed in prairie hay meadows in eastern Kansas and Oklahoma in the spring. The species is also a popular ornamental.

Finger coreopsis (*C. palmata* Nutt.) is often found in similar habitats in the eastern quarter of the region. It has 3-parted leaves and stiffly erect stems.

Tragopogon dubius Scop.

Goat's beard,
Western salsify

Asteraceae
Sunflower Family

Description
Goat's beard is an erect, smooth or unevenly hairy, biennial or short lived perennial 1–3½ ft. tall, with milky sap and
a long taproot. Stems are 1 to several,
sometimes branched, and hollow. Leaves
are alternate, simple, sessile, entire,
linear, 4–16 in. long, and mostly less
than ¼ in. wide. Heads are solitary, cylindrical, and borne at the ends of long
stalks that are slightly swollen just below
the heads. Bracts on the heads are 13,
linear, and longer than the florets; florets
are numerous, pale yellow, and all raylike. Fruiting heads are spherical, with
recurved bracts; fruits* are cylindrical,
slightly ribbed, beaked, tan achenes up

to 1½ in. long, with an umbrella-like
cluster of slender, grayish, feathery
bristles at the tip.

Blooming Period
May–July.

Habitat
Disturbed sites, including prairies, pastures, roadsides, fields, and waste areas;
throughout region.

The common name is a reference to the
feathery bristles at the tip of the achenes.
The fruiting heads can be preserved for
short-term use in dried-flower arrangements by spraying them with clear
acrylic before carefully picking them.
    Salsify, or vegetable oyster (*T. porrifo-
lius* L.), has purple florets and is widely
scattered throughout the region. Both
species yield edible roots and were introduced from Europe.

...nnia pinnatifida A. Gray

...mann's daisy

Asteraceae
Sunflower Family

Description
Engelmann's daisy is an erect or spreading, stiffly hairy perennial ½–2 ft. tall. Stems are single or often clustered, arising from a woody taproot. Leaves are alternate, stalked or the upper ones sessile, pinnately lobed, 4–10 in. long, and ½–3 in. wide. Inflorescences are 1–1½ in.–wide heads in loose clusters on long stalks arising from near the ends of stems. Bracts of the heads are in several series and linear to lance-shaped; ray florets are usually 8, yellow, and about ½ in. long; disk florets are numerous and yellow. Fruits are flattened egg-shaped achenes with several short scales at the tip.

Blooming Period
May–August.

Habitat
Open mixed and shortgrass prairies, especially over limestone; W ½.

Engelmann's daisy is a very common late-spring- and summer-flowering composite. It is the only species in the genus.

Hymenoxys scaposa (DC.) Parker

Plains hymenoxys

Asteraceae
Sunflower Family

Description
Plains hymenoxys is a tufted, smooth to sparingly hairy but never silky, perennial herb, without obvious stems; it arises from a tough woody rootstock. Leaves are basal, simple, sessile or short-stalked, linear to narrowly lance-shaped, 1–4 in. long, and less than ¼ in. wide, with entire margins and densely hairy leaf bases. Inflorescences are solitary on erect naked stalks 2–12 in. long. Bracts on the heads are thin and silky; ray florets are yellow, up to ¾ in. long, and 4-nerved; disk florets are also yellow. Fruits are short dark achenes with short scales at the tip.

Blooming Period
May–July, sometimes also in September–October.

Habitat
Open, rocky, mixed and shortgrass prairies, usually on limestone; W ⅔.

Plains hymenoxys often occurs with stemless hymenoxys [*H. acaulis* (Pursh) Parker]. The latter is a silky-hairy, tufted, perennial herb with naked flowering stems and numerous basal leaves.

Hymenoxys odorata DC.

Bitterweed

Asteraceae
Sunflower Family

Description

Bitterweed is an erect, aromatic, smooth to sparingly hairy, annual herb that grows up to 1½ ft. tall, with a taproot. Stems are bushy-branched. Leaves are alternate, mostly sessile, numerous, 1–4 in. long, and deeply pinnately divided, with 3–15 threadlike lobes. Heads are numerous, solitary, and produced at the ends of branches or on stalks arising from leaf bases. Bracts on the heads are less than ¼ in. long; ray florets are 6–13, yellow, up to ½ in. long, and prominently 3-toothed at the tip; disk florets are also yellow. Fruits are short, dark, hairy achenes with short scales at the tip.

Blooming Period
May–August.

Habitat
Dry, open shortgrass prairies, especially in heavily grazed areas with limestone soils; SW ¼.

Bitterweed occasionally forms large, showy stands in dry washes and pastures. It is poisonous to livestock.

Opuntia macrorhiza Engelm.

Plains prickly pear

Cactaceae
Cactus Family

Description

Plains prickly pear is a low, spreading, spiny cactus usually less than ⅓ ft. tall. Stem segments are padlike, blue-green, waxy, flattened, egg-shaped to elliptic or rounded, 2–5 in. long, 2–4 in. wide, bearing clusters of few to many stout straight or slightly twisted spines* up to 2 in. long. Leaves are absent. The showy yellow or yellowish red flowers are 1 to several at the ends of pads, broadly funnel-shaped, and 2–3 in. wide; stamens are numerous, with yellow or reddish filaments. Fruits* are fleshy, red or purple, egg-shaped berries up to 2 in. long and contain numerous pale flattened seeds.

Blooming Period
May–August.

Habitat
Dry rocky prairies of all types; throughout region.

Large, dense populations are often observed on grazed shortgrass prairies. Tree cholla [*O. imbricata* (Haw.) DC.] is a tree-like plant with cylindrical stems up to 10 ft. tall and pink or reddish purple flowers. It is scattered to locally common in the western third of our region. Little prickly pear [*O. fragilis* (Nutt.) Haw.] is seldom over 6 in. tall and has barbed spines and egg-shaped stem segments that detach easily. It occurs in the northwestern quarter and rarely flowers. Fruits of opuntias are edible, as are the despined pads.

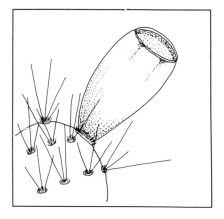

Mimulus glabratus H.B.K. var. *fremontii* (Benth.) A.L. Grant

Roundleaf monkey-flower

Scrophulariaceae
Figwort Family

margins. Flowers are solitary on stalks up to 1½ in. long arising from the bases of upper leaves. The calyx is 5-lobed with the lobes unequal; the corolla is prominently 2-lipped, with 2 upper lobes and 3 lower lobes, yellow, often red-spotted, up to ½ in long, and hairy at the throat; stamens are 4, in 2 sets of different lengths. Fruits are egg-shaped capsules about ¼ in. long and contain numerous small brownish seeds.

Blooming Period
May–August.

Habitat
Still and slowly flowing shallow water in and along streams, rivers, ponds, and springs; scattered throughout region.

Description
Roundleaf monkey-flower is a low, creeping, smooth to sparsely glandular-hairy, aquatic, perennial herb 2–12 in. tall, often tinged reddish and rooting at the nodes. Stems are 1 to several, weak, and sometimes branched. Leaves are opposite, simple, short-stalked below to sessile and clasping above, rounded to kidney-shaped, ½–1 in. long and ¼–1 in. wide, with entire to shallowly toothed

The common name is a fanciful reference to the resemblance of the flower to a face. Sharpwing monkey-flower (*M. alatus* Ait.) and Alleghany monkey-flower (*M. ringens* L.) are erect blue-flowered species found in the eastern quarter of the region. The former has stalked leaves and flowers on stalks about ½ in. long; the latter has sessile leaves and flower stalks sometimes longer than 1 in.

Asclepias tuberosa L.

Butterfly milkweed,
Pleurisy root

Asclepiadaceae
Milkweed Family

Description

Butterfly milkweed is a perennial herb 1–3 ft. tall, with few to many stems arising from a woody rootstock. Stems are long-hairy and mostly unbranched and contain watery sap. Leaves are alternate, simple, crowded, velvety beneath but mostly hairless and shiny green above, 2–4 in. long, ¼–1 in. wide, and lance-shaped with short stalks. Inflorescences are 1 to many umbels produced at or near the ends of the stems. Each umbel contains 6–25 hairy flowers, which are 5-parted with greenish sepals, bright orange, red, or yellow petals, and similarly colored hoods and horns. Fruits are hairy pods 3–6 in. long that contain nu-merous seeds, each with a tuft of long white hairs at the tip.

Blooming Period

May–August.

Habitat

Sandy, loamy, or rocky limestone tall-grass and mixed prairies; E ⅔.

This exceedingly attractive species is the only milkweed in the region without milky sap. Cultivated forms are available for gardens. The common names refer to the plant's attractiveness to butterflies and the use of its roots by Indians to treat pleurisy.

Linum sulcatum Ridd.

Grooved flax

Linaceae
Flax Family

rounded to egg-shaped, 10-segmented capsules containing few small brownish seeds.

Blooming Period
May–September.

Habitat
Tallgrass and mixed prairies and open woods; E ½.

Common flax (*L. usitatissimum* L.) is a blue-flowered European species cultivated for linen fiber and linseed oil. It was introduced and grown in the eastern quarter of our region in the late nineteenth century; however, the plants do not persist long outside of cultivation.

Description
Grooved flax is an erect, smooth, slender, annual herb ¾–3 ft. tall, with a slender taproot. Stems are simple and branched above the middle. Leaves are alternate, simple, sessile, entire, usually with small glands at the base, linear to narrowly lance-shaped, ½–1 in. long, and less than ⅛ in. wide. Flowers are borne in open, terminal, panicle-like clusters; sepals are 5 and glandular-toothed; petals are 5, pale yellow, and less than ½ in. long and fall readily from the plant; there are 5 stamens. Fruits* are smooth,

Psilostrophe villosa Rydb.

Paperflower

Asteraceae
Sunflower Family

Description

Paperflower is an erect, woolly, perennial herb ½–2 ft. tall, with a taproot. Stems are several to many, with stiff spreading branches. Leaves are alternate, simple, stalked below to sessile above, gradually reduced up the stem, and spatula-shaped to elliptic; the basal leaves usually are abundant and matted, ½–4 in. long, ⅛–¾ in. wide, and entire or 3- to 5-lobed. Inflorescences are numerous small congested clusters of heads at the ends of branches. Bracts on the heads are densely woolly and narrowly lance-shaped; ray florets are 3–4, golden yellow, ¼ in. long, and 3-lobed to 4-lobed at the tip; disk florets are 5–12 and golden yellow. Fruits are smooth, short, linear achenes with 4–6 narrowly lance-shaped scales at the tip.

Blooming Period

May–September.

Habitat

Mixed, shortgrass, and sandsage prairies, often in sandy sites; SW ¼.

Melilotus officinalis (L.) Lam.

Yellow sweet clover

Fabaceae
Bean Family

Description

Yellow sweet clover is an erect, smooth to sparsely hairy, annual or biennial herb 1–6 ft. tall, with a long taproot. Stems are slender and branched. Leaves are alternate and stalked, with 3 lance-shaped to narrowly elliptic leaflets ½–1½ in. long, less than ½ in. wide, and toothed along the margins. Inflorescences are loose, slender, 1–4 in.–long racemes on short stalks arising from the bases of leaves, mostly toward the ends of branches. Flowers are yellow, almost ¼ in. long, and 5-parted; there are 10 stamens, 9 joined by their filaments and 1 free. Fruits are small, smooth, brown, egg-shaped legumes containing a single seed.

Blooming Period

May–September.

Habitat

Disturbed sites, including roadsides, fields, and waste areas; throughout region.

The sweet fragrance of *Melilotus* persists after it is dried. The species has various medicinal uses. When sweet clover hay gets moldy, a toxic substance is formed that poisons cattle.

Caesalpinia jamesii (T. & G.) Fisher

James rush-pea

Caesalpiniaceae
Caesalpinia Family

to yellow-orange, and about ¼ in. long; the 10 stamens have hairy filaments. Fruits* are flat, glandular, crescent-shaped legumes containing 2–3 shiny seeds.

Blooming Period
May–September.

Habitat
Shortgrass, mixed, and sandsage prairies in rocky, gravelly, or sandy soil, often where disturbed; W ½.

James rush-pea is very similar to Indian rush-pea [*Hoffmanseggia glauca* (Ort.) Eifert] but may be distinguished by the presence of bright orange glands on the leaves and stems and the lighter-colored flowers.

Description
James rush-pea is a perennial herb covered with distinctive orange glands that dry black and a stout, branched, woody rootstock. Stems are usually several, branched above, and ¼–1½ ft. tall. Leaves are alternate, hairy beneath, stalked, and twice-pinnately compound, with 5–7 segments, each with 5–10 pairs of egg-shaped leaflets. Inflorescences are racemes of 3–15 flowers arising from the bases of upper leaves. The calyx is 5-lobed and hairy; the petals are 5, yellow

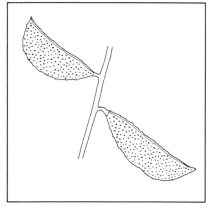

Hoffmanseggia glauca (Ort.) Eifert

Indian rush-pea,
Pignut

Caesalpiniaceae
Caesalpinia Family

hairy, and glandular; petals are 5 and about ½ in. long; the 10 stamens are red with hairy filaments. Fruits* are flat, glandular, sickle-shaped legumes 1–1½. in. long and contain several brownish seeds.

Blooming Period
May–September.

Habitat
Dry, rocky to sandy, shortgrass prairies, floodplains, pastures, fields, roadsides, and other disturbed sites; SW ⅓.

Indian rush-pea is a noxious weed in Kansas because of its aggressive nature and tubers that are difficult to eliminate once established.

Description
Indian rush-pea is a bluish green perennial herb, with a well-developed creeping rootstock bearing small nutlike tubers. Stems are spreading or erect, sometimes branched, and ¼–1½ ft. tall; the upper portions bear stalked glands. Leaves are alternate, stalked, and odd-bipinnate, with 3–7 segments, each with 6–11 pairs of elliptic leaflets. Inflorescences are terminal racemes of 5–15 yellow-orange to red-orange flowers. The calyx is 5-lobed,

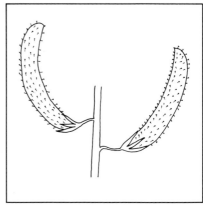

Ludwigia peploides (H.B.K.) Raven

Floating evening primrose

Onagraceae
Evening Primrose Family

Blooming Period
May–October.

Habitat
Shallow water and muddy flats around ponds, lakes, streams, and ditches; E ½.

Bushy seedbox (*L. alternifolia* L.) is an erect perennial that grows up to 3 ft. tall, with 4-parted stalked flowers. It occurs on moist prairies and along streams, rivers, and marshes in the eastern half of our region.

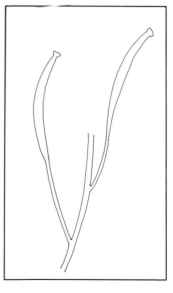

Description
Floating evening primrose is a floating or creeping, smooth, aquatic, perennial herb. Stems are ½–2 ft. long, usually branched, and often rooting at the nodes in land forms. Leaves are alternate, simple, stalked, entire, spatula-shaped to elliptic or lance-shaped, ½–4 in. long, and ¼–1½ in. wide. Flowers are solitary on stalks up to 2½ in. long, arising from the bases of upper leaves; the calyx is 5-lobed; the bright yellow corolla is 5-lobed and up to 1 in. long; there are 10 stamens. Fruits* are smooth to sparsely hairy cylindrical capsules up to 1½ in. long and contain numerous small seeds.

Physalis longifolia Nutt.

Common ground cherry

Solanaceae
Nightshade Family

Description
Common ground cherry is an erect, smooth to short-hairy, perennial herb ½–2 ft. tall. Stems are usually single, branched above, and purplish and arise from a deep rhizome. Leaves are alternate, simple, stalked, lance-shaped to ovate, 1–6 in. long, and ½–3 in. wide, with entire to wavy margins. Flowers are drooping on stalks about ½ in. long arising from the bases of leaves. The calyx is 5-lobed; the pale yellow corolla is funnel-shaped with 5 angular lobes, and the throat is brownish or bluish brown; there are 5 stamens. Fruits* are yellow, many-seeded berries enclosed by a papery lanternlike calyx.

Blooming Period
May–October.

Habitat
All prairie types, open woods, stream valleys, roadsides, and disturbed sites; throughout region.

The eight species of *Physalis* in the region are often difficult to distinguish. Hair type is critical in separating the species. Virginia ground cherry (*Physalis virginiana* P. Mill.) is found in similar habitats and has the same range as common ground cherry. It is identified by the presence of downward-directed hairs on the stem.

Several species of *Physalis*, also called "husk tomatoes" because of the persistent husklike calyx, are cultivated for their edible fruits. At least one species is also grown as an ornamental.

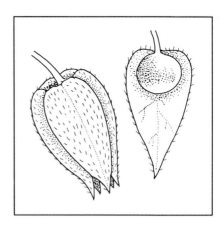

Solanum rostratum Dun.

Buffalo bur,
Kansas thistle

Solanaceae
Nightshade Family

and shallowly funnel-shaped, bright yellow, and ½–1 in. wide; stamens are 5, with 4 yellow and 1 brownish to purplish, curved, and longer. Fruits* are spherical berries containing abundant dark seeds and surrounded by the enlarged prickly calyx.

Blooming Period
May–October.

Habitat
Disturbed sites, including prairies, pastures, fields, feedlots, roadsides, and waste areas; throughout region.

This hardy, aggressive, drought-tolerant weed is known to most people who live in the Great Plains. When it dies, the stem breaks off and the plant behaves much like a tumbleweed, scattering seeds as it rolls along in the wind.

Description
Buffalo bur is an erect annual herb ½–2½ ft. tall, covered with tiny star-shaped hairs and abundant, straight, yellowish prickles. Stems are single, multi-branched, and yellowish green. Leaves are alternate, stalked, elliptic to egg-shaped in outline but 1–2 times pinnately lobed, 1–5 in. long, ½–3½ in. wide, and green above but yellowish green beneath. Inflorescences are short racemes of 5–15 stalked flowers arising near the ends of branches. The calyx is 5-lobed and densely covered with yellow prickles; the corolla is 5-angled, flattened

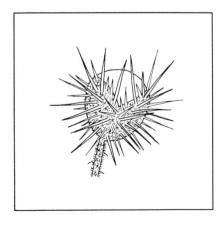

Tribulus terrestris L.

Puncture vine,
Goat head

Zygophyllaceae
Caltrop Family

Description
Puncture vine is a low, spreading, hairy, annual herb with a taproot; it often forms dense mats. Stems are simple, multi-branched from the base, and up to 5 ft. long. Leaves are opposite, short-stalked, ½–2 in. long, and even-pinnately compound, with 3–7 pairs of elliptic to egg-shaped, ¼ in.–long and ⅛ in.–wide, entire leaflets. Flowers are solitary and borne on short stalks arising from the bases of leaves; sepals are 5, about ⅛ in. long, and hairy; the 5 yellow petals are egg-shaped and up to ¼ in. long; there are 10 stamens. Fruits* are dry, about ½ in. wide, and 5-segmented, each segment bearing 2–4 stout spines, few to many shorter spines or bumps, and few small seeds.

Blooming Period
May–October.

Habitat
Disturbed sites and waste areas; throughout region.

Livestock that eat puncture vine may develop hypersensitivity to sunlight.
 The Caltrop Family is a small group of mostly subshrubs and small trees, abundant in arid tropical and subtropical regions. Creosote bush [*Larrea tridentata* (DC.) Cov.], a common shrub in the desert Southwest, is among the better-known members of this family.

Haplopappus spinulosus (Pursh) DC.

Cutleaf ironweed

Asteraceae
Sunflower Family

ous and also yellow. Fruits are small, appressed-hairy achenes with yellowish brown bristles at the tip.

Blooming Period
May–October.

Habitat
Most prairie types, but infrequently on tallgrass prairies, also pastures and road-sides, generally in sandy to gravelly soil; W ⅔.

This is a highly variable species through-out its range, with several phases repre-sented in the southern Great Plains.

Description
Cutleaf ironweed is a minutely glandular-hairy perennial herb 1–2½ ft. tall, with a woody rootstock. Stems are erect or spreading, usually numerous, and often branched. Leaves* are alter-nate, sessile, crowded, egg-shaped to spatula-shaped, ½–2½ in. long, mostly less than ¼ in. wide, and toothed or pin-nately divided into narrow lobes, with bristles on the teeth or lobes. Heads are roughly ½ in. wide and mostly solitary at the ends of branches. Bracts on the heads are linear and tipped with short bristles; ray florets are 15–30, ½ in. long, and yellow; disk florets are numer-

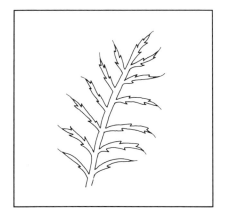

Thelesperma megapotamicum (Spreng.) O. Ktze.

Slender greenthread

Asteraceae
Sunflower Family

Description
Slender greenthread is an erect, slender, smooth, perennial herb 1–3 ft. tall, arising from a creeping woody rootstock. Stems are 1 to several and branched above. Leaves are opposite, short-stalked to sessile, 1–4 in. long, simple to deeply pinnately divided, with linear segments about ⅛ in. wide. Heads are solitary, bell-shaped, up to ¾ in. wide, and borne at the ends of stalks 3–9 in. long. Bracts on the heads are narrowly egg-shaped and united at the base; ray florets are absent; disk florets are orangish yellow and numerous. Fruits are slender, slightly flattened, reddish brown achenes about ¼ in. long and tipped with 2 triangular barbed bristles.

Blooming Period
May–October.

Habitat
Nearly all prairie types, pastures, and roadsides, particularly in rocky limestone soil; W ¾ and infrequent in E ¼.

Greenthread [*T. filifolium* (Hook.) A. Gray] has golden-yellow ray florets and urn-shaped heads. It occurs throughout the southern two-thirds of our region and may be mistaken for bigflower coreopsis (*Coreopsis grandiflora* Hoog ex Sweet). However, the latter has bracts on the heads that are not united and flat winged achenes.

Zinnia grandiflora Nutt.

Rocky Mountain zinnia

Asteraceae
Sunflower Family

Description
Rocky Mountain zinnia is a low, tufted, perennial herb ¼–1 ft. tall. Stems are appressed-hairy, branched, and several to many and arise from a woody rootstock. Leaves are opposite, simple, mostly linear, up to 2 in. long, and covered with small glands. Inflorescences are numerous heads at the ends of stems and up to 1½ in. wide. Ray florets are 3–6, pale to deep yellow, with a papery texture; disk florets are more numerous, small, and orange to red. Fruits are small angular achenes topped by short bristles.

Blooming Period
May–October.

Habitat
Open, dry shortgrass prairies, especially in limestone soil; SW ¼.

This attractive composite will form large patches of flowers that readily catch the eye. The species is frequently found on rocky slopes in our region.

Zinnia elegans Jacq., a native of Mexico, is widely cultivated and available in many colors. The genus honors eighteenth-century German botanist Johann Gottfried Zinn.

Cucurbita foetidissima H.B.K.

Buffalo-gourd,
Wild gourd

Cucurbitaceae
Cucumber Family

Description
Buffalo-gourd is a coarse, spreading, perennial herb that often forms dense leafy
mats with a distinctive gray-green color.
Stems are up to 10 ft. long and arise
from a thick woody root. Leaves are alternate, simple, stalked, rough, triangular
egg-shaped to heart-shaped, 4–12 in.
long, 3–10 in. wide, with irregularly
spaced teeth along the margins. Large
showy flowers are borne singly at the
bases of leaves; male and female flowers
are produced on the same plant, with
male flowers on long stalks and female
flowers sessile; the calyx is 5-parted; the
corolla is trumpetlike, 5-lobed, deep yellow to orange, and up to 5 in. long; there
are 5 stamens. Fruits* are spherical,
green and white striped, and 3–4 in. in

diameter; each gourd contains many
smooth flattened seeds.

Blooming Period
June–August.

Habitat
Sandy to gravelly or rocky prairies, pas-
tures, disturbed sites, and waste areas;
W ¾.

Cucurbita is a small genus of New World
plants. It includes several species grown
for their edible fruits, such as field
pumpkin (*C. pepo* L.), winter crookneck
squash (*C. moschata* Duchn.), and winter
squash (*C. maxima* Duchn.).

Campsis radicans (L.) Seem.

Trumpet-creeper,
Trumpet-vine

Bignoniaceae
Bignonia Family

Description
Trumpet-creeper is a climbing or sprawling, woody, perennial vine. Leaves are opposite, mostly smooth, stalked, up to 1 ft. long and 6 in. wide, and odd-pinnately compound, with 5–13 lance-shaped toothed leaflets. Inflorescences are groups of 5–15 large showy flowers. The fleshy calyx is 5-lobed and reddish green and bears small glands; the corolla is orange to reddish orange, leathery, tubular, and inflated, 2–3½ in. long, 2-lipped, with 2 upper lobes and 3 lower lobes that typically are reddish orange or red; there are 5 stamens, one of which is sterile. Fruits* are drooping cylindrical capsules 5–8 in. long with tapering ends and contain abundant flattened 2-winged seeds.*

Blooming Period
June–September.

Habitat
Roadsides, fencerows, thickets, and stream banks; E ⅓.

The Bignonia Family consists mostly of tropical and subtropical trees and shrubs known for their large showy flowers. Trumpet-creeper is among the few temperate members. Indian cigar tree (*Catalpa speciosa* Warder) is a popular ornamental member that occasionally escapes from cultivation in our region.

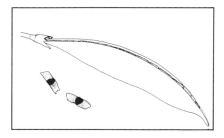

Verbascum thapsus L.

Common mullein,
Flannel mullein

Scrophulariaceae
Figwort Family

Description
Common mullein is an erect, stout, densely woolly, biennial herb 1–7 ft. tall, with a large taproot. Stems are single and infrequently branched above. Leaves are alternate, simple, sessile, and entire; the basal ones are 2–20 in. long and 1–5 in. wide and form a large rosette; stem leaves are gradually reduced upward, with leafy wings extending downward from the leaf bases. Inflorescences are crowded, terminal, wandlike spikes. The calyx is densely hairy and 5-lobed; the yellow corolla is shallowly funnel-shaped, 5-lobed, ½–1¼ in. wide, with spreading lobes; there are 5 stamens, the upper 3 with hairy filaments. Fruits* are rounded to egg-shaped capsules over ¼

in. long and contain numerous tiny, brown, ridged seeds.

Blooming Period
June–September.

Habitat
Disturbed sites, including fields, pastures, roadsides, and waste areas; NE ½.

This Eurasian immigrant has been used to treat a wide range of human maladies, and the leaves have been a source of yellow-green dye. Moth mullein (*V. blattaria* L.), also introduced from the Old World, occurs primarily in the eastern third of the region. It is slender and mostly smooth; flowers are yellow or white with reddish centers; all five stamens are hairy; and fruits are rounded capsules on stalks. Fruiting spikes are attractive in dried arrangements.

Dalea aurea Nutt. ex Pursh

Golden prairie-clover

Fabaceae
Bean Family

stalked, ½–1½ in. long, ½–1 in. wide, and odd-pinnately compound, with 3–9 lance-shaped leaflets. Inflorescences are crowded, many-flowered, conelike spikes produced at the ends of stems. The 5-lobed calyx is silky; the 5 petals are bright yellow; there are 10 stamens joined by their filaments. Fruits are short silky legumes containing a single yellowish seed.

Blooming Period
June–September.

Habitat
Nearly all types of prairie, often on gravelly ridges and rocky slopes, and occasionally on wooded slopes; W ⅔.

Description
Golden prairie-clover is an erect, silky-hairy, perennial herb ¾–2½ ft. tall. Stems are 1 to several and occasionally branched above and arise from a stout yellow taproot. Leaves are alternate,

James' dalea [*D. jamesii* (Torr.) T. & G.] is a short yellow-flowered species with 3 leaflets and branched woody stems and rootstocks. It occurs on rocky shortgrass prairies in the southwestern quarter of our region.

Coreopsis tinctoria Nutt.

Plains coreopsis

Asteraceae
Sunflower Family

Description
Plains coreopsis is an erect glabrous annual 2–4 ft. tall. Stems are single from a taproot and typically multi-branched above. Leaves are opposite, 1–4 in. long, and pinnately or twice-pinnately compound, with linear segments. Heads are ½–1 in. wide, numerous, and at the ends of short stalks near the ends of branches. Bracts on the heads are narrowly lance-shaped to triangular; ray florets are 7–9, up to ½ in. long, yellow with a prominent reddish spot at the base, and conspicuously toothed at the tip; disk florets are 4-lobed and reddish.

Fruits are black wingless achenes with no bristles or scales.

Blooming Period
June–September.

Habitat
Wet or seasonally wet sites, including ditches, roadsides, fields, and disturbed areas; throughout region.

Plains coreopsis often forms dense yellow stands in wet ditches and fields. It is also a popular ornamental and a source of yellow, brown, and reddish dyes.

Ratibida columnifera (Nutt.) Woot. & Standl.

Yellow prairie coneflower

Asteraceae
Sunflower Family

and sometimes branched. Leaves are alternate, stalked, 1–5 in. long, up to 3 in. wide, and pinnately divided and occasionally twice so, with unequal linear segments. Inflorescences are 1 to several columnar heads up to 2 in. long and borne at the ends of long stalks. Ray florets are 4–11, golden yellow or purplish brown, up to 1 in. long, and usually drooping; disk florets are purplish brown and abundant. Fruits are short, gray, flattened, mostly smooth achenes tipped with 1–2 spikelike bristles.

Blooming Period
June–September.

Habitat
All prairie types, roadsides, and waste areas; throughout region.

Description
Yellow prairie coneflower is an erect, appressed-hairy, gland-dotted, perennial herb ½–4 ft. tall, arising from a stout taproot. Stems are 1 to several, ribbed,

Grayhead prairie coneflower [*R. pinnata* (Vent.) Barnh.] is a tall fibrous-rooted plant found on tallgrass prairies and in thickets and open woods in the eastern quarter of our region.

Lactuca ludoviciana (Nutt.) Ridd.

Western wild lettuce

Asteraceae
Sunflower Family

Description

Western wild lettuce is an erect, smooth, biennial herb 3–6 ft. tall, with brownish milky sap. Stems are single and usually unbranched except above. Leaves are alternate, simple to pinnately lobed, sessile and sometimes clasping, prickly along the vein of the lower leaf surface, egg-shaped, 8–12 in. long, and 2–4 in. wide, with toothed margins. Inflorescences are many cylindrical heads borne in open panicles at the ends of branches. Ray florets are 20–30 and yellow to pale blue; disk florets are absent. Fruits are flattened, egg-shaped, brown achenes with a slender beak at the tip bearing numerous slender white bristles.

Blooming Period

June–September.

Habitat

Most prairie types, roadsides, and disturbed sites; E ¾.

Garden lettuce (*L. sativa* L.) has been selected for large basal leaves and less sap production. However, clear evidence of its kinship to other lettuces can be seen if plants are allowed to flower. Prickly lettuce (*L. serriola* L.) is a widespread weed with short-spiny achenes.

Rudbeckia hirta L.

Black-eyed Susan

Asteraceae
Sunflower Family

Description

Black-eyed Susan is an erect, coarsely spreading-hairy, biennial or short-lived perennial herb 1–3½ ft. tall, with fibrous roots. Stems are 1 to several and typically branched. Leaves are alternate, simple, stalked to sessile, and gradually reduced up the stem; basal leaves are lance-shaped to elliptic, 2–7 in. long, ½–2 in. wide, and nearly entire to shallowly toothed. Inflorescences are few to many 2–3 in.–wide heads on long stalks at the ends of branches. Bracts on the heads are spreading-hairy; ray florets are 8–21, yellow-orange to yellow, and 1–1½ in. long; disk florets are numerous and brownish purple. Fruits are short, dark, 4-angled achenes without scales or bristles.

Blooming Period

June–September.

Habitat

Tallgrass and mixed prairies, roadsides, pastures, and waste areas; E ½ and widely scattered in W.

Brown-eyed Susan (*R. triloba* L.) has smaller heads than black-eyed Susan, brownish-purple disk florets, and nearly smooth entire or 3-lobed leaves. It is found in moist, open, sunny places in the eastern quarter of our region. Golden glow (*R. laciniata* L.) is a tall, mostly smooth perennial with yellow disk florets and 3-lobed to 5-lobed leaves. It also occurs in the eastern quarter in moist places, often along stream banks and in open woods. Several species of *Rudbeckia* have medicinal uses and can be sources of yellow dye.

Silphium laciniatum L.

Compass plant

Asteraceae
Sunflower Family

Description
Compass plant is an erect, coarse, sparingly stiff-hairy, resinous, perennial herb 3–10 ft. tall, with a massive woody rootstock. Stems are usually single, unbranched, and stiff. Leaves are alternate, stiff, long-stalked below but sessile above, gradually reduced up the stem, deeply pinnately divided with the segments mostly linear and bearing a few large teeth; basal leaves are prominent, up to 1½ ft. long and 1 ft. wide. Inflorescences are elongate and racemelike, with large bell-shaped heads 2–4 in. wide. Bracts on the heads are egg-shaped; ray florets are yellow, numerous, and up to 1½ in. long; disk florets are also yellow and numerous. Fruits are broad flattened achenes about ½ in. long, with a notch at the tip.

Blooming Period
June–September.

Habitat
Tallgrass and mixed prairies, roadsides, and slightly disturbed sites, especially in rocky soil; E ½.

The common name refers to the tendency for leaves of the plant to be oriented with the edges of the blades pointing north and south. Cup rosinweed (*S. perfoliatum* L.) is robust and square-stemmed and has prominent, clasping leaves. It is found on low wet ground along rivers, streams, and ditches in the eastern quarter of our region.

Silphium integrifolium Michx.

Whole-leaf rosinweed

Asteraceae
Sunflower Family

Description

Whole-leaf rosinweed is an erect, coarse, smooth to rough, somewhat resinous, perennial herb 1½–5 ft. tall, with a woody rootstock. Stems are 1 to several, stiff, and mostly unbranched. Leaves are mostly opposite, simple, sessile and often clasping, egg-shaped to lance-shaped, 3–6 in. long, and 1–2½ in. wide, with entire to toothed margins. Inflorescences are short terminal clusters with few 2–4 in.–wide bell-shaped heads. Bracts on the heads are egg-shaped; ray florets are yellow, numerous, and up to 1½ in. long; disk florets are also yellow and numerous. Fruits are broad flattened achenes about ½ in. long, with a notch at the tip.

Blooming Period

June–October.

Habitat

Tallgrass and mixed prairies, roadsides, and disturbed sites, especially in moist rocky soils; E ½.

Plants in the eastern quarter of our region tend to be persistently hairy and are referred to as var. *integrifolium*. At drier sites, especially in the western part of the region, plants are less hairy and sometimes waxy. These plants, referred to as var. *laeve* T. & G., are treated as *S. speciosum* Nutt. in many earlier works.

Abutilon theophrasti Medic.

Velvetleaf

Malvaceae
Mallow Family

Habitat
Fields, pastures, roadsides, and disturbed sites; E ½.

Introduced from eastern Asia, velvetleaf is a well-established weed throughout much of eastern North America. The attractive fruits can be used in dried arrangements or wreaths. This species is cultivated in China and the Soviet Union as a source of fibers. "China jute" is used for sacks, twine, fishing nets, and mats.

Description
Velvetleaf is an erect annual herb ½–6 ft. tall and covered with soft, velvety, star-shaped hairs. Stems are slightly sticky and typically branched. Leaves are alternate, simple, velvety, 2–7 in. long, 2–6 in. wide, and broadly heart-shaped, with long stalks. Flowers are 5-parted, up to 1 in. across, and scattered on stalks from the bases of the upper leaves; the petals are yellow to yellow-orange; the many stamens are united into a central column. Fruits* are capsule-like with numerous segments, each containing 2 or more flat, black, heart-shaped seeds.

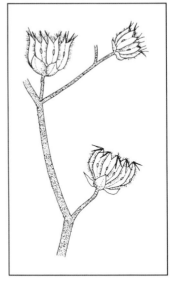

Blooming Period
June–October.

Cassia chamaecrista L.

Showy partridge pea

Caesalpiniaceae
Caesalpinia Family

mottling at the base; the 10 stamens are yellow or purple and unequal in size. Fruits* are flat, brown, linear-oblong legumes containing 4–10 small dark seeds.

Blooming Period
June–October.

Habitat
Rocky and sandy prairies, fields, open woods, and roadsides; E ⅔.

Maryland senna (*C. marilandica* L.), a perennial relative with large flowers, is found in the eastern half of our region. It generally occupies wetter sites than those favored by showy partridge pea. Flowers of both species keep their golden color after being pressed. The seeds of some species of *Cassia* are eaten by wild birds.

Description
Showy partridge pea is an erect summer annual, with short appressed hairs. Stems are slender, often branched, and ¼–4 ft. tall. Leaves are alternate, stalked, and once-pinnately compound, with 8–15 pairs of linear-oblong leaflets. Inflorescences are few-flowered racemes arising from the bases of leaves. Flowers are showy, with 5 lance-shaped sepals; the 5 golden-yellow petals are unequal in size, with the lower one over ½ in. long and curved and the upper 4 smaller with red

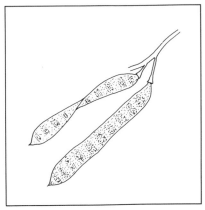

Hypericum perforatum L.

Common St. John's-wort

Clusiaceae
St. John's-wort Family

Description
Common St. John's-wort is an erect, smooth, often colonial, perennial herb 1–2½ ft. tall, with well-developed rhizomes. Stems are several to many, ridged, and often branched. Leaves* are opposite, simple, sessile, covered with numerous transparent dots, linear to elliptic, 1–1½ in. long, and less than ¾ in. wide, with entire margins. Inflorescences are few to many leafy-bracted dense clusters of flowers borne at the ends of branches. Sepals are 5; petals are 5, yellow, and up to ½ in. long and bear black dots along the margins; stamens are numerous and clustered into 3 groups. Fruits* are egg-shaped capsules containing many small, dark, pitted seeds.

Blooming Period
June–October.

Habitat
Disturbed sites, including pastures, prairies, roadsides, and waste areas; scattered in E ½.

This European introduction is a troublesome weed in parts of the western United States but rarely in the Great Plains. Livestock that eat it become hypersensitive to sunlight and develop dermatitis. The flowers yield a yellow dye. This plant often blooms on St. John's Day in Europe.

Roundfruit St. John's-wort (*H. sphaerocarpum* Michx.) is a native species without black dots on the petals, many free stamens, and rounded fruits. It occurs in the eastern quarter of our region. Spotted St. John's-wort (*H. punctatum* Lam.) is found in the same area; it has black dots on the petals and undersides of leaves and free stamens.

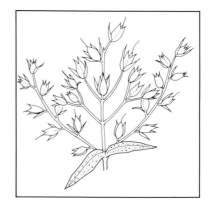

Mentzelia oligosperma Nutt.

Stickleaf,
Stickleaf mentzelia

Loasaceae
Stickleaf Family

Description
Stickleaf is a spreading to erect, coarse, rough-hairy, perennial herb ½–3 ft. tall, with a large taproot. Stems are 1 to several, multi-branched, and whitish. Leaves are alternate, simple, sessile, narrowly egg-shaped to somewhat diamond-shaped, ½–2½ in. long, and ¼–1 in. wide, with coarsely toothed margins. Inflorescences are solitary flowers or few-flowered clusters borne near the ends of branches. Flowers are about ¾ in. wide and open in the morning; sepals are 5 and lance-shaped; the 5 petals are about ¼ in. long and pale yellow to orange; stamens are 15–40 and about as long as the petals. Fruits are cylindrical to club-shaped capsules up to ½ in. long and contain 1–4 winged seeds.

Blooming Period
June–October.

Habitat
Dry rocky prairies, rocky road cuts, and occasionally pastures; scattered throughout region.

The common name refers to the tenacious manner in which leaves stick to clothing or fur.

Oenothera rhombipetala Nutt. ex T. & G.

Fourpoint evening primrose

Onagraceae
Evening Primrose Family

Description

Fourpoint evening primrose is a soft-hairy annual or biennial herb 1–4 ft. tall, arising from a taproot. Stems are erect and often spreading-branched from the base. Leaves are alternate, simple, mostly sessile, crowded, lance-shaped to narrowly egg-shaped, gradually reduced up the stem, ½–4 in. long, and mostly less than ¾ in. wide, with entire or toothed margins; basal leaves are often larger and wavy-margined. Inflorescences are dense, many-flowered, terminal spikes up to 1 ft. long. Flowers are showy and open around sunset; sepals are 4 and reflexed; petals are 4, yellow, diamond-shaped, up to 1 in. long, and at the end of a 1–2 in.–long floral tube; stamens are 8. Fruits are tapered, curved, ½–1 in.–long capsules containing many small, pitted, reddish brown seeds.

Blooming Period

June–October.

Habitat

Sand prairies, stream valleys, roadsides, and disturbed sites; C ⅓.

Oenothera biennis L.

Common evening primrose

Onagraceae
Evening Primrose Family

mens are 8. Fruits* are hairy cylindrical capsules up to 1½ in. long and contain many small angular seeds.

Blooming Period
July–October.

Habitat
Open, disturbed sites, including fields, pastures, roadsides, and damp areas; throughout region except SW ¼.

Spikes of capsules are attractive additions to dried arrangements.

Description
Common evening primrose is a tall, erect, hairy, biennial herb 1½–7 ft. tall, arising from a taproot. Stems are single and spreading-branched. Leaves are alternate, simple, long-stalked below to sessile above, often red-spotted, 2–12 in. long, and ½–3 in. wide, with entire to toothed margins. Inflorescences are short to long, sometimes congested, terminal spikes. Flowers are numerous and open around sunset; sepals are 4 and reflexed; petals are 4, yellow, ½–1 in. long, and at the end of a 1–2 in.–long floral tube; sta-

Helianthus annuus L.

Common sunflower

Asteraceae
Sunflower Family

Description
Common sunflower is an erect annual herb 2–10 ft. tall. Stems are stiff, rough-hairy, and often branched above. Leaves* are mostly alternate, simple, stalked, egg-shaped to triangular, 4–16 in. long, 2–10 in. wide, with an entire or toothed and hairy margin. Inflorescences are heads 3–6 in. across, with 1 to several borne at the ends of stems or from the bases of leaves; there may be several dozen heads per plant. Bracts on the heads are narrowly to broadly triangular; ray florets are yellow and 1–2 in. long; disk florets are numerous and reddish brown to purple. Fruits are flattened achenes with 2 bristles at the tip.

Blooming Period
July–September.

Habitat
Open, disturbed sites and prairies; throughout region.

Plains sunflower (*Helianthus petiolaris* Nutt.) is similar to common sunflower, and both species frequently occupy disturbed habitats. Plains sunflower typically is shorter in stature and has smaller heads; the tiny bracts situated among the disk florets each bear a conspicuous tuft of white hairs at their tip.

The large-headed plants grown commercially in the Great Plains were developed from common sunflower. They are drought resistant and yield valuable oil and edible kernels.

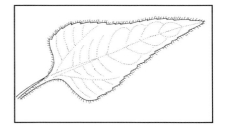

Helianthus rigidus (Cass.) Desf.

Stiff sunflower

Asteraceae
Sunflower Family

Description
Stiff sunflower is an erect, rough-hairy, perennial herb 1–6 ft. tall. Stems are few-branched, often reddish, and arise from a stout rhizome. Leaves* are generally opposite, simple, stalked or the upper ones sessile, narrowly lance-shaped to egg-shaped, 2–12 in. long, 1–2½ in. wide, rough, and entire to toothed. Heads are 3–4 in. wide and single or few on long stalks at the ends of stems. Bracts on the heads are lance-shaped or broader; ray florets are 10–20, 1–1½ in. long, and yellow; disk florets are reddish purple to yellow with red lobes. Fruits are achenes with 2 prominent slender bristles and smaller scales at the tip.

Blooming Period
July–September.

Habitat
Dry, upland, tallgrass and mixed prairies and roadsides; E ½.

Ashy sunflower (*H. mollis* Lam.) is frequently found on upland prairies with stiff sunflower. It has sessile heart-shaped leaves, white-woolly hairs, and yellow disk florets.
   Sunflowers were probably named for their resemblance to the sun with rays of light projecting from it. They do tend to face the sun, but so do many other flowers.

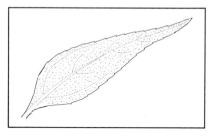

Helianthus grosseserratus Martens

Sawtooth sunflower

Asteraceae
Sunflower Family

loose groups. Bracts on the heads are linear to narrowly lance-shaped; ray florets are 10–20, 1–2 in. long, and yellow; disk florets are numerous and yellow. Fruits are short achenes with 2 scales at the tip.

Blooming Period
July–October.

Habitat
Wet draws in tallgrass prairies, openings along rivers and streams, meadows, fields, ditches, and roadsides; E ⅓.

Jerusalem artichoke (*H. tuberosus* L.) occurs in habitats similar to those of sawtooth sunflower throughout the eastern two-thirds of our region. It has mostly opposite, egg-shaped or broadly lance-shaped leaves and well-developed edible tubers along a rhizome.

Description
Sawtooth sunflower is an erect perennial herb 3–12 ft. tall, with a tough woody root. Stems are often smooth and waxy below but appressed-hairy above. Leaves* are mostly alternate, simple, stalked, rough above and hairy beneath, lance-shaped, 4–10 in. long, 1–3 in. wide, and usually sharply toothed. Heads are few to many, 3–4 in. wide, and in

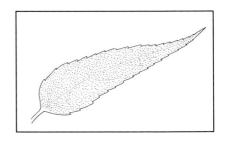

Helianthus maximilianii Schrad.

Maximilian sunflower

Asteraceae
Sunflower Family

Description
Maximilian sunflower is an erect, rough-hairy, perennial herb 2–10 ft. tall. Stems are single or clustered from a thick rhizomatous rootstock. Leaves* are mostly alternate, simple, short-stalked, lance-shaped, typically folded lengthwise, 2½–12 in. long, and ½–2 in. wide, with entire to slightly toothed margins and both surfaces rough-hairy to minutely hairy. Heads usually are numerous, 3–4 in. wide, and in racemelike clusters. Bracts on the heads are linear to lance-shaped; ray florets are 10–25, 1–2 in. long, and yellow; disk florets are also yellow. Fruits are small, brown and gray, mottled achenes without bristles or scales.

Blooming Period
July–October.

Habitat
A variety of prairie types, in ditches, along roadsides, and in disturbed sites; E ¾.

Because it has edible kernels and an apparent ability to control weeds, Maximilian sunflower is being studied as a potential crop.

Willow-leaved sunflower (H. salicifolius A. Dietr.) is common on limestone tallgrass prairies in the eastern third of our region. It has very long narrow leaves and reddish disk florets.

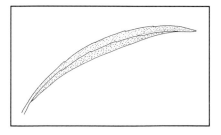

Grindelia squarrosa (Pursh) Dun.

Curly-top gumweed,
Curly-cup gumweed

Asteraceae
Sunflower Family

Description
Curly-top gumweed is a spreading to erect, sticky, biennial herb ¼–4 ft. tall. Stems are usually single and short-branched, especially above. Leaves are alternate, simple, sessile and clasping, gland-dotted, spatula-shaped to egg-shaped, ½–3 in. long, and less than ¾ in. wide, with entire to coarsely toothed margins. Inflorescences are several to many heads 1–1½ in. wide and borne at the ends of branches. Bracts on the heads are resinous, with strongly recurved tips; ray florets are yellow, up to ½ in. long, but occasionally absent; disk florets are also yellow. Fruits are short, ribbed achenes tipped with 2–8 slender toothed bristles.

Blooming Period
July–October.

Habitat
Disturbed sites, including prairies, pastures, roadsides, and waste areas; N ½ and scattered in S.

Curly-top gumweed quite predictably can be observed at the edge of asphalt along our highways. Hot summer days are not good times to get to know this plant because the sticky resin can quickly deter even the most-persistent plant collector or wildflower enthusiast.

Dyssodia papposa (Vent.) Hitchc.

Fetid marigold

Asteraceae
Sunflower Family

Description
Fetid marigold is an erect or spreading, mostly smooth, annual herb ¼–1½ ft. tall and covered with abundant orange, translucent, oil glands.* Stems are mostly single but multi-branched from the base. Leaves* are mostly opposite, sessile or short-stalked, ½–2 in. long. ½–1½ in. wide, and simple to deeply pinnately divided, with toothed margins. Inflorescences are small, cylindrical, sessile or short-stalked heads borne near the ends of branches. Bracts on the heads are 6–12 and glandular; ray florets are 5–13, inconspicuous, and yellow to orange; disk florets are 12–50 and brownish yellow. Fruits are short, stout, hairy achenes with scales at the tip.

Blooming Period
July–October.

Habitat
Disturbed sites, including fields, pastures, roadsides, and waste areas, especially in shallow rocky soil; throughout region.

Fetid marigold is usually smelled before it is seen. As the common name implies, the plant has the pungent odor of marigolds, which is particularly noticeable when it is crushed.

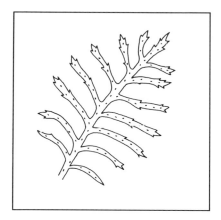

Solidago canadensis L.

Canada goldenrod

Asteraceae
Sunflower Family

Description
Canada goldenrod is an erect, hairy, pe-rennial herb 1–6 ft. tall. Stems are mostly unbranched, 1 to several, and arise from creeping rhizomes. Leaves* are alternate, simple, short-stalked to sessile, gradually reduced up the stem, 3-nerved, narrowly lance-shaped to elliptic, 1–6 in. long, and ¼–¾ in. wide, with shallowly toothed margins; lower leaves typically are absent on flowering plants. Inflores-cences are open to dense, terminal, panicle-like clusters of tiny cylindrical heads; lower branches usually have heads on the upper side only. Bracts on the heads are thin and yellowish with a greer tip; ray florets are 5–18, yellow, and less than ⅛ in. long; disk florets are 2–8 and yellow. Fruits are tiny short-hairy achenes with numerous white bristles at the tip.

Blooming Period
July–October.

Habitat
Nearly all prairie types, thickets, open woods, and open disturbed sites; throughout region.

This highly variable goldenrod is among the most common and widely distributed in the region. Giant goldenrod or late goldenrod (*S. gigantea* Ait). is similar to Canada goldenrod but has smooth stems below the inflorescences. It also occurs throughout the region, mostly in moist sites. Goldenrods have various medicinal uses and produce pale yellow to orange-yellow dyes, depending on the mordant.

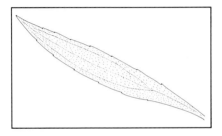

Solidago missouriensis Nutt.

Missouri goldenrod

Asteraceae
Sunflower Family

branches arch noticeably and have heads on the upper side only. Bracts on the heads are firm and rounded, ray florets are 7–13, yellow, and about ⅛ in. long; disk florets are 8–13 and yellow. Fruits are tiny smooth to sparingly hairy achenes tipped with numerous white bristles.

Blooming Period
July–October.

Habitat
Nearly all prairie types and roadsides; throughout most of region except SW ¼.

Goldenrods are often disdained by botanists and wildflower enthusiasts because they can be exceedingly difficult to identify. This is because many species tend to intergrade. Fewer than a dozen species occur in our region. Inflorescences can be air-dried for winter arrangements; a light coating of hair spray or clear acrylic spray will prevent the developing achenes from separating.

Description
Missouri goldenrod is an erect, smooth, perennial herb 1–3 ft. tall. Stems are generally unbranched and single or clustered from creeping rhizomes. Leaves* are alternate, simple, mostly sessile, gradually reduced up the stem, somewhat thick, 3-nerved, linear to lance-shaped or elliptic, 2–5 in. long, and ¼–1 in. wide, with entire to toothed margins; lower leaves are usually absent on flowering plants. Inflorescences are open to dense, terminal, panicle-like clusters of small cylindrical heads; the lower

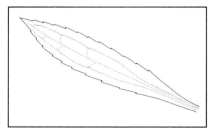

Solidago rigida L.

Rigid goldenrod

Asteraceae
Sunflower Family

Description

Rigid goldenrod is an erect, rough-hairy, perennial herb ½–5 ft. tall, with a stout branched rootstock. Stems are usually unbranched and clustered. Leaves* are alternate, simple, long-stalked below to sessile above, firm, and gradually reduced up the stem; basal leaves are prominent, lance-shaped to broadly egg-shaped, 2–10 in. long, and 1–4 in. wide, with entire to obscurely toothed margins. Inflorescences are dense, terminal, flattened or rounded clusters of bell-shaped heads. Bracts on the heads are firm and rounded; ray florets are 7–14, yellow, and about ¼ in. long; disk florets are 20–30 and yellow. Fruits are smooth ribbed achenes tipped with slender white bristles.

Blooming Period
August–October.

Habitat
Tallgrass, mixed, and occasionally short-grass prairies, especially in dry rocky soil; NE ½.

Soft goldenrod (*S. mollis* Bartl.) is grayish green with spreading hairs, a panicle-like inflorescence, 4–8 ray florets, and hairy achenes. It is found in the western two-thirds of our region. Showy-wand goldenrod (*S. speciosa* Nutt.) and downy goldenrod (*S. petiolaris* Ait.) occur in the eastern quarter and the eastern half, respectively. Both have smooth achenes and flowering branches with heads borne on both sides. Showy-wand goldenrod has leaves gradually reduced up the stem and rounded bracts on the heads. By contrast, downy goldenrod has leaves roughly equal in size up the stem and pointed bracts on the heads.

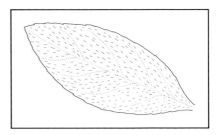

Heterotheca latifolia Buckl.

Camphor weed

Asteraceae
Sunflower Family

Description
Camphor weed is an erect, sticky, aromatic, annual or biennial herb ¾–5 ft. tall, with a taproot. Stems are single but usually multi-branched above. Leaves are alternate, simple, stalked below to sessile and clasping above, gradually reduced up the stem, narrowly egg-shaped to elliptic, ½–3 in. long, and ¼–2 in. wide, with entire or sparingly toothed margins. Inflorescences are few to many ½–1 in.– wide heads on short stalks near the ends of branches. Bracts on the heads are linear, sticky, and straw-colored, with a green midrib; ray florets are many, yellow, and less than ¼ in. long; disk florets are also yellow. Fruits are somewhat angular achenes; those of the disk florets are hairy and tipped with short scales and longer bristles.

Blooming Period
July–October.

Habitat
Open sandy prairies, roadsides, pastures, and disturbed sites; S ½ and into N-C ⅓.

Haplopappus ciliatus (Nutt.) DC.

Wax goldenweed

Asteraceae
Sunflower Family

flowering plant. Heads are roughly 1 in. wide and solitary or few in open clusters at the ends of stems. Bracts on the head are narrowly lance-shaped, with spreading or recurved tips; ray florets are 25–50, about ½ in. long, and waxy yellow; disk florets are also yellow. Fruits are small, somewhat flattened achenes with yellowish-brown rigid bristles at the tip.

Blooming Period
August–October.

Habitat
Dry, open, sandy to rocky, disturbed sites and waste areas; C ⅔.

Description
Wax goldenweed is a smooth erect annual 1–4 ft. tall. Stems are single from a taproot. Leaves* are alternate, simple, sessile and clasping, thickish, egg-shaped, 1–3 in. long, and ½–1½ in. wide, with toothed margins, each tooth tipped with a short bristle; leaves typically are absent on the lower third of the

Senecio riddellii T. & G.

Riddell ragwort

Asteraceae
Sunflower Family

Description
Riddell ragwort is an erect, smooth, perennial subshrub 1–3 ft. tall, with a woody rootstock. Stems are numerous, branched, and woody at the base. Leaves are alternate, stalked to sessile, often crowded, pinnately lobed with linear segments, and up to 4 in. long and 3 in. wide. Heads are many, up to 1¼ in. wide, cylindrical to bell-shaped, and on long stalks in flat-topped terminal clusters. Ray florets are mostly 8, light yellow to yellow, and over ¼ in. long; disk florets are yellow and numerous. Fruits are cylindrical, ribbed, short-hairy, gray achenes with abundant slender white bristles at the tip.

Blooming Period
August–October.

Habitat
Mixed, shortgrass, and sandsage prairies, rocky pastures, and roadsides; W ½.

This plant is toxic to livestock, and in the past, concerted efforts were made to eliminate the species from pastures. Other ragworts are also known to be poisonous.

Woolly ragwort (*S. douglasii* DC.) is widespread, occurring from the southwestern quarter of the region west to California and south into Mexico. It is shrubby and grayish and has woolly stems and leaves.

Gutierrezia dracunculoides (DC.) Blake

Broomweed

Asteraceae
Sunflower Family

rowly lance-shaped, ½–2½ in. long, and less than ⅛ in. wide, with entire margins. Inflorescences are many small urn-shaped or top-shaped heads clustered near the ends of branches. Ray florets are 7–9, yellow, and less than ¼ in. long; disk florets are also yellow. Fruits are tiny, dark, minutely hairy achenes produced only by the ray florets.

Blooming Period
August–October.

Habitat
Open disturbed prairies, pastures, roadsides, and waste areas, especially on limestone; throughout region except NW ¼, and most abundant in E.

Description
Broomweed is an erect, smooth, annual herb ½–3 ft. tall, with a slender taproot. Stems are single and multi-branched in the upper half of the plant, with slender, spreading branches. Leaves are alternate, simple, sessile, resinous, linear to nar-

Dried plants are popular in fall flower arrangements. It is not uncommon to find massive populations in heavily grazed pastures. The common name refers to the use of the plant by European settlers, who tied dense bundles of dried plants to sticks and used them as brooms.

Gutierrezia sarothrae (Pursh) Britt. & Rusby

Broom snakeweed

Asteraceae
Sunflower Family

Description

Broom snakeweed is a spreading to erect, smooth to sparingly hairy, perennial herb or subshrub. Stems are several to many, usually branched, and occasionally resinous and arise from a woody rootstock. Leaves are alternate, simple, sessile, threadlike to linear, ¼–2½ in. long, and less than ⅛ in. wide, with entire margins. Inflorescences are abundant small cylindrical or top-shaped heads borne in clusters at the ends of branches. Ray florets are 3–8, yellow, and less than ⅛ in. long; disk florets are 2–6 and yellow. Fruits are short, tan to brown, short-hairy achenes tipped with 8–10 white to yellowish scales.

Blooming Period

August–October.

Habitat

Open, dry, mixed and shortgrass prairies; W ½.

Broom snakeweed essentially replaces broomweed [*G. dracunculoides* (DC.) Blake] in the western part of the region. It is also often abundant in heavily grazed prairies. This species was used as a treatment for snakebite.

Bidens frondosa L.

Beggar-ticks

Asteraceae
Sunflower Family

Description
Beggar-ticks is a slender, smooth to sparingly hairy, annual herb ½–3½ ft. tall. Stems are sometimes tinged reddish. Leaves are opposite, stalked, 2–8 in. long, and pinnately divided, with 3–5 narrow toothed segments. Heads are numerous, about ½ in. across, and produced on short to long stalks arising from the bases of leaves. Ray florets, when present, are less than ¼ in. long; disk florets are yellow-orange. Fruits* are flattened dark brown or black achenes with 2 hooked bristles at the top.

Blooming Period
August–October.

Habitat
Wet open areas along rivers, streams, ponds, and ditches, in disturbed sites, and in open wet woods; throughout region except SW ¼.

Nodding beggar-ticks (*B. cernua* L.) has a distribution similar to that of beggar-ticks but has simple leaves. Spanish needles (*B. bipinnata* L.) is a common weed throughout the eastern two-thirds of our region. Like beggar-ticks, it has pinnate leaves and lacks ray florets. However, the achenes of Spanish needles are long, spindle-shaped, and tipped with 3–4 bristles.

The small hooked achenes of *Bidens* are the bane of many a sportsperson and nature lover. However, they provide a highly effective means of fruit dispersal.

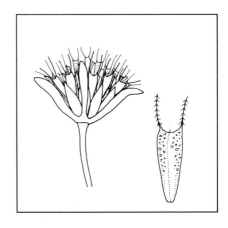

Verbesina alternifolia (L.) Britt.

Wingstem

Asteraceae
Sunflower Family

Description
Wingstem is an erect, rough-hairy, perennial herb ½–8 ft. tall, with a woody rootstock. Stems are usually branched above and have leafy wings extending down from the leaf bases. Leaves are alternate, simple, short-stalked, 4–10 in. long, and 1–3 in. wide, with nearly entire to toothed margins. Inflorescences are numerous heads borne in open terminal clusters. Bracts on the heads are few, narrowly lance-shaped, and reflexed in fruit; ray florets are 10–15, yellow, usually drooping, and up to 1 in. long; disk florets are yellow and spreading. Fruits are flat, smooth, winged, spreading achenes with 2 short stiff bristles at the tip.

Blooming Period
August–October.

Habitat
Open moist woods, stream banks, and bottomlands; E ⅓.

Three other species of *Verbesina* occur in the region; however, none is common.

Helenium autumnale L.

Sneezeweed

Asteraceae
Sunflower Family

Description
Sneezeweed is an erect, smooth to finely hairy, perennial herb 1–4 ft. tall, with a fibrous rootstock. Stems are 1 to several, branched above, and with leafy wings extending down from the leaf bases. Leaves are alternate, simple, sessile, numerous, narrowly lance-shaped to elliptic, 1½–6 in. long, and ½–1½ in. wide, with toothed margins. Heads are several to many and borne in open leafy clusters at the ends of branches. Bracts on the heads are very narrow; ray florets are 10–20, yellow, ½–1 in. long, prominently 3-toothed at the tips, and often drooping; disk florets are yellow, abundant, and borne in dense spherical clusters. Fruits are short, dark, appressed-hairy achenes tipped with 5 lance-shaped scales.

Blooming Period
August–October.

Habitat
Damp areas on prairies, along rivers, streams, and ponds, and in ditches; E ¼.

Sneezeweed is reported to be poisonous to livestock. The odor of this plant is supposed to cause sneezing.

Bitter sneezeweed [*H. amarum* (Raf.) Rock] is a bushy-branched annual found in disturbed sites, pastures, and fields, predominantly in the southeastern quarter of our region. Plants occasionally form dense stands.

Glossary

Achene A dry 1-seeded fruit that does not open at maturity.

Alternate Placed singly one above the other on alternate sides of the stem.

Annual A plant that completes its life cycle in 1 year or less.

Anther The pollen-bearing part of a stamen.

Barbed Having spinelike hooks that bend backward sharply.

Beak A long, slender, firm point.

Beard Long stiff hairs arranged in a row or tuft.

Biennial A plant that completes its life cycle in 2 years.

Bract A modified or reduced leaf.

Bristle A stiff hair.

Bulb An underground bud with fleshy scales.

Calyx The outer series of flower parts, composed of the sepals and usually green.

Capsule A dry fruit with several sections that open.

Clasping Partly or completely surrounding the stem (as the base of a sessile leaf).

Column A group of united filaments.

Compound Composed of 2 or more similar parts.

Corm A fleshy bulb-like base of a stem, usually underground.

Corolla The inner series of flower parts, composed of the petals and usually colored.

Disk floret A small tubular flower in the central portion of a head (the Sunflower Family).

Elliptic Oval in shape.

Fibrous Resembling or composed of fibers.

Filament The stalk of a stamen supporting the anther.

Flower The reproductive portion of a plant, usually composed of sepals, petals, stamens, and a pistil.

Fruit The ripened ovary of a flowering plant, containing seeds.

Gland A secretory organ.

Habit The general appearance of a plant.

Head A short dense cluster of small flowers, usually sessile.

Herb A plant lacking persistent woody parts aboveground.

Herbaceous Having the character of a herb.

Hood An erect to spreading petal-like structure with incurved margins (in some flowers of the Milkweed Family).

Horn A curved appendage protruding from the hood (in some flowers of the Milkweed Family).

Inflorescence The flowering portion of a plant.

Leaf A flat outgrowth of a stem capable of manufacturing food and usually green.

Leaflet One part of a compound leaf.

Legume A dry fruit usually opening into 2 parts and containing 1 row of seeds (the Bean Family).

Lobe A rounded partial division of a plant part.

Midrib The central vein of a leaf.

Nut A hard 1-seeded fruit that does not open.

Nutlet A small nut.

Opposite Arranged in pairs on opposite sides of a stem.

Palmate Divided in a handlike manner.

Panicle A branched inflorescence with stalked flowers.

Perennial A plant that lives 3 or more years.

Perfect A flower with both stamens and pistils.

Petal One part of the corolla (usually colored).

Pinnate A compound leaf with leaflets arranged on both sides of the stalk; odd-pinnate has a terminal leaflet, and even-pinnate lacks a terminal leaflet.

Pistil The female reproductive structure of a flower consisting of an ovary-bearing ovules, a style, and a sticky stigma that receives pollen.

Pitted Having tiny indentations on the surface.

Pod A dry fruit that opens along the sides.

Prickle A small sharp outgrowth on a surface.

Raceme An inflorescence, often elongate, with stalked flowers.

Ray floret A straplike small flower in the outer portion of a head (the Sunflower Family).

Recurved Curved backward or outward.

Reflexed Abruptly bent or curved downward.

Resin An organic secretion not soluble in water.

Rhizome An underground stem, usually lateral and producing shoots and roots.

Root An underground organ that anchors a plant in the soil and absorbs water and nutrients.

Rootstock An underground part resembling a rhizome.

Rosette A compact circle of plant parts.

Scale A thin, dry, flat plant part, usually a leaf or bract.

Sepal One part of the calyx (usually green).

Sessile Lacking a stalk.

Sheath A tubular structure surrounding part of an organ.

Shrub A persistent woody plant with several stems from the base.

Spike An inflorescence, often elongate, with sessile flowers.

Spur A hollow tubular projection from a petal or sepal, usually containing nectar.

Stalk The slender supporting structure of an organ.

Stamen The male reproductive structure of a flower, consisting of a filament and anther.

Stipule An appendage at the base of a leaf stalk.

Stolon A horizontal aboveground stem that forms roots at intervals.

Style The usually elongated portion of the pistil between the ovary and stigma.

Taproot The primary descending root of a plant.

Tendril A slender twisting organ by which a plant clings to a support.

Tuber A thickened, short, below-ground stem that serves as a storage organ.

Tufted Closely clustered stems.

Umbel A rounded or flat-topped inflorescence with flowers on stalks that arise from a common point.

Vine A plant with long flexible stems trailing on the ground or climbing on other plants.

Whorl Arrangement of plant parts in a circle.

Wing A thin membranelike extension of a plant part.

Woolly Covered with curly soft hairs, usually matted.

References

Anderson, Kling L., and Clenton E. Owensby. *Common names of a selected list of plants*. Manhattan: Kansas Agricultural Experiment Station. Technical Bulletin 117. 1969.

Bare, Janet E. *Wildflowers and weeds of Kansas*. Lawrence: Regents Press of Kansas. 1979.

Barkley, T. M. *Field guide to the common weeds of Kansas*. Lawrence: University Press of Kansas. 1983.

Denison, Edgar. *Missouri wildflowers*. Jefferson City: Missouri Department of Conservation. 1978.

Embertson, Jane. *Pods: Wildflowers and weeds in their final beauty*. New York: Charles Scribner's Sons. 1979.

Great Plains Flora Association. *Atlas of the flora of the Great Plains*. Ames: Iowa State University Press. 1977.

——— . *Flora of the Great Plains*. Lawrence: University Press of Kansas. 1986.

Kindscher, Kelly. *Edible wild plants of the prairie: An ethnobotanical guide*. Lawrence: University Press of Kansas. 1987.

Küchler, A. W. *Potential natural vegetation of the conterminous United States*. American Geographical Society Special Publication 36. New York: American Geographical Society. 1964.

Lommasson, Robert C. *Nebraska wild flowers*. Lincoln: University Press of Nebraska. 1973.

Loughmiller, Campbell, and Lynn Loughmiller. *Texas wildflowers: A field guide*. Austin: University of Texas Press. 1985.

Martin, William C., and Charles R. Hutchins. *Spring wildflowers of New Mexico*. Albuquerque: New Mexico Natural History Survey, University of New Mexico Press. 1984.

——— . *Fall wildflowers of New Mexico*. Albuquerque: New Mexico Natural History Survey, University of New Mexico Press. 1988.

Owensby, Clenton E. *Kansas prairie wildflowers*. Ames: Iowa State University Press. 1980.

Runkel, Sylvan T., and Dean M. Roosa. *Wildflowers of the tallgrass prairie: The upper Midwest*. Ames: Iowa State University Press. 1989.

Stephens, H. A. *Poisonous plants of the Central United States*. Lawrence: Regents Press of Kansas. 1980.

Vance, Fenton R., James R. Jowsey, and James S. McLean. *Wildflowers of the northern Great Plains*. Minneapolis: University of Minnesota Press. 1984.

Index

This index includes all plant names mentioned in the introduction (except those used only as examples of Latin words), keys, descriptions, and discussions. Latin family, genus, and species names are in italics.